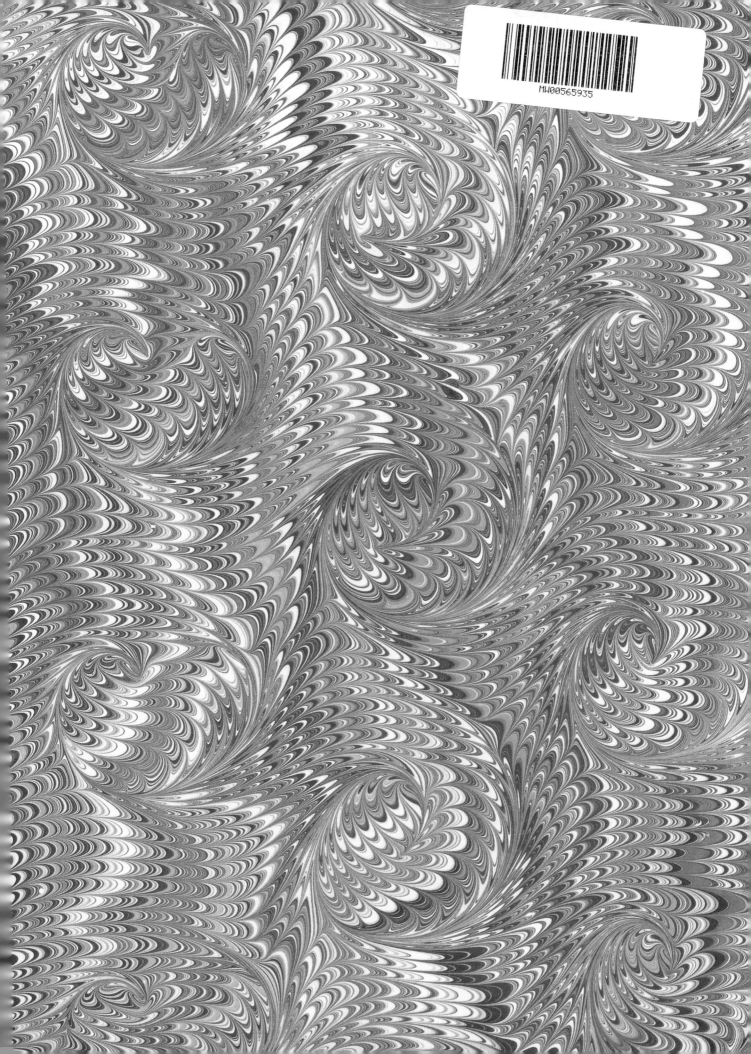

Noritake for Europe

Pat Murphy

4880 Lower Valley Road, Atglen, PA 19310 USA

Designed by John P. Cheek
Cover design by Bruce M. Waters
Type set in University Roman Bd BT/Dutch 801 Rm BT

ISBN: 0-7643-1354-1
Printed in China
1 2 3 4

Published by Schiffer Publishing Ltd.
4880 Lower Valley Road
Atglen, PA 19310
Phone: (610) 593-1777; Fax: (610) 593-2002
E-mail: Schifferbk@aol.com
Please visit our web site catalog at
www.schifferbooks.com
We are always looking for people to write books on new
and related subjects. If you have an idea for a book
please contact us at the above address.

This book may be purchased from the publisher.
Include $3.95 for shipping.
Please try your bookstore first.
You may write for a free catalog.

In Europe, Schiffer books are distributed by
Bushwood Books
6 Marksbury Ave.
Kew Gardens
Surrey TW9 4JF England
Phone: 44 (0) 20 8392-8585; Fax: 44 (0) 20 8392-9876
E-mail: Bushwd@aol.com
Free postage in the U.K., Europe; air mail at cost.

Contents

A cknowledgments

I should like to provide just a few acknowledgments to those people who have made a major contribution to this work. To Mr. Toshiaki Suzuki, Managing Director of Noritake (UK) Ltd., who has taken the time and trouble to answer many questions for me, and given me the benefit of his knowledge and experience. To David Spain of Seattle, Washington, USA, whose superb books on Noritake have inspired me and whose support throughout this project has been freely given, to the extent of providing an interesting and thought provoking foreword for this book. My heartfelt thanks to you both. To those members of the Noritake Collector's Club (UK) who have opened their homes and collections to our camera to allow me to include many new pictures, my warm appreciation of their generosity, with special thanks to Jean & Terry Beddows, Chris & Margaret Dales, Herb & Gerry Clowes, and Merv Preston and his wife.

And, finally, to my wife, Jane, and my son, Andrew, who have spent the last months as a combination of editors, photographers, proof readers, and valuers in addition to their day jobs as very busy Noritake dealers, my deep love and gratitude for endless patience, uncomplaining support, and believing that I could do it.

F oreword

By David Spain

Noritake for Europe is a terrific book and also unique. It is the first and only book dedicated to the discussion and display of Noritake collectibles originally exported to Great Britain and Europe. More than that, it is a much-needed book because, in a very real sense, it "completes the set." With Noritake for Europe plus the similarly Schiffer-published "A to Z" Noritake books, the various books on "Nippon" and some important but so far not well known Japanese books on "Old Noritake," dealers and collectors can finally see, at one sitting, just how astonishing the Noritake Company's product line was during the first half of the twentieth century. Although a book on European Noritake has long been needed, it is only thanks to Pat Murphy's efforts that we now have it. For that, all Noritake collectors and dealers are happily in his debt.

Since there are, as has just been indicated, quite a few books on the products of the Noritake Company and since "European" Noritake has been presented in most of these books, I think it may be useful to offer a few more comments about the need for this book. One reason the book is needed is that, until now, published materials on European Noritake have been rather limited in scope and, for the most part, have been scattered widely in these sources. To make matters worse, many of these books are not readily available, are in Japanese (which, alas, most native speakers of English do not read), or are titled in a way that could lead them to be overlooked by collectors or dealers who define themselves as being interested in "Noritake." In the latter category are Joan Van Patten's very important "Nippon" books.

Even in my own books on Noritake collectibles, which were meant to be comprehensive and that at least have the virtue of using the word "Noritake" in their titles, one will find relatively few items with backstamps indicating that the pieces originally were exported to non-North American countries (e.g., to Great Britain primarily, but also to Australia, New Zealand, and, in a book in press, to India). This was not, I hasten to add, the result of a lack of interest or the application of a restrictive organizational or collecting principle. There is only one reason so few items from that part of the range are shown in my books: lack of photographs.

With these facts in mind, it can be seen why Pat Murphy's book is so useful. He has access to photographic materials that, for all practical purposes, are simply unavailable here. Moreover, as an active collector of and respected dealer in European Noritake collectibles for over ten years, he knows the field like no other. And now, with the vital and able assistance of his wife Jane and son Andrew, he has recently formed the Noritake Collectors Club (UK) Ltd. In conjunction with this he has begun to publish an impressive new quarterly newsletter entitled "Noritake" (the first issue was distributed in January 2000). As a consequence, he was and is uniquely positioned to put together the beautiful book you now hold in your hands.

Noritake for Europe is valuable for yet another reason. To explain it, we must begin by taking note of an admittedly rather obvious historical fact: different countries and governments at different times have required that different words about the origin of those goods be placed on those goods. This fact has ramifications that quietly continue to shape the interests and activities of hundreds of collectors to this very day. Of the many regulatory details that might be considered in this context, two in particular loom large. In Great Britain, Noritake goods imported as early as 1908 had backstamps containing both the word "Japan" and "Noritake." This was essentially the opposite of requirements in the United States. With virtually no exceptions, the words "Noritake" and "Japan" do not appear on Noritake Company products imported to the United States until 1921. Indeed, except for Noritake green ware shipped to the United States for use by hobbyist decorators, even the word "Noritake" alone was uncommon. Since collectors in North America generally agree that the Noritake Company must have decorated an item in order for it to be considered a "Noritake collectible," they generally do not collect these items and they are not presented in books on Noritake collectibles.

One consequence of this is that rather different thoughts and images come to mind when collectors and dealers in different parts of the world hear the word "Noritake." The many ideas that people have, however, can be compressed into two broad viewpoints, one found in Japan and Great Britain and the other being rather widespread among collectors in North America. In Great Britain and Japan, respectively, the word "Noritake" and the phrase "Old Noritake" designate virtually all decorative ceramic (mostly porcelain) products made for home use by the Noritake Company from about 1891 until around 1939. This is because virtually all of the Noritake materials imported by Great Britain have backstamps with the words "Noritake" and "Japan" in them. (Again, there is an interesting exception, namely Australia and New Zealand, where the backstamps often had no words at all.)

Although the range of items available in Japan and Great Britain, then or now, was not the same, the material now of interest to collectors covers a very wide range of styles. Quite simply, this is because the Noritake Company produced items with decoration in whatever style was fashionable over this time period. The styles range from European-inspired nineteenth century formal or "classical" motifs to several more contemporary looks from the Arts and Crafts movement to Art Nouveau and Art Deco. To be sure, collectors in Great Britain and Japan vary in their preferences within this range, just as collectors everywhere do. Moreover, it is becoming increasingly clear that the materials exported to Great Britain and to various places in the Commonwealth (Australia, India, and New Zealand) were not the same as those that were being exported to North America. In addition, from books published in Japan, we are beginning to discover that the Noritake Company made a rather distinct line of decorative and giftware (or fancy line) products for their domestic (non-export) market. But, on the whole, i.e., taking "Noritake (or "Old Noritake") collectors" as a group in these two areas, the word "Noritake" includes collecting interests that range over the entire gamut of styles seen during the first half of·the twentieth century.

In North America, on the other hand, the situation is very different. The stylistic range of the things collected by these "Noritake collectors" is very great. Indeed, if one can imagine measuring such a thing, it may be as great as it is in Japan and Great Britain. The range is not, however, the same in North America as it is in Japan and Great Britain. One can most easily see this by considering the two ranges in chronological terms. In Great Britain and Japan, as has just been noted, the time period covered is from about 1891 to about 1939. In North America, on the other hand, the time period designated by the term "Noritake" is from about 1921 to about 1955.

This difference is largely the result of a change in regulations in the United States pertaining to the way the country of origin should be recorded on imported goods. Prior to 1921, goods from Japan destined for the United States used the word "Nippon" for the name of the country of origin and usually did not include the

English language version of the name of the company that had manufactured the item. Out of this fact has grown another one: in North America, collectors of ceramics made by the Noritake Company have formed two groups, both in the formal and informal senses of the term. The older of the two groups, by approximately a decade, is the International Nippon Collectors Club (INCC). The other group is the Noritake Collectors Society (NCS). Most members of the NCS are primarily interested in decorative fancy line or giftware ceramics (generally porcelain) if they bear backstamps known to be Noritake Company marks. Indeed, for many North American Noritake collectors, there is a marked preference for items with backstamps that state explicitly that the item was made in "Japan" (not in "Nippon") by the Noritake Company.

In the INCC, on the other hand, the focus is on porcelains from a country and an era. The country, of course, is Japan; the era was the period from 1891 to 1921. For years, as a consequence, most INCC members happily focused their collecting energies on ceramic items with backstamps containing the word "Nippon" (the country name). The fact that the items were made by different companies was (and still is) essentially irrelevant. In general, this approach by the INCC has worked very well. By any measure, the INCC must be reckoned as one of the best collector's clubs anywhere and Van Patten's many books on Nippon era porcelains are virtually without peer in the collecting world.

From time to time, however, INCC members were faced with some interesting anomalies. Classically, these were Japanese porcelains which, in terms of style, seemed clearly to be of the Nippon era but which had backstamps that not only lacked the word "Nippon," but also and, for some, more significantly, contained the word "Noritake." Should Nippon Club members collect them? Well, these questions were answered eventually (it took many years) when the INCC declared, quite reasonably in my view, that certain backstamps (a) without the word "Nippon" but (b) with the word "Noritake" were in fact used during the "Nippon Era." Consequently, items bearing such backstamps could be of legitimate interest to collectors of and dealers in Nippon era porcelains. The form and decoration of the piece would determine the issue, not the presence or absence of particular words. In short, the INCC was saying that it should be the style of the piece that matters. I applaud the INCC for taking this stand.

To some, of course, this may seem obvious and not worth discussing. In North America at the time, however, more than a few expert Nippon collectors and dealers were convinced that Nippon-marked items were far superior in materials and/or workmanship to porcelains containing the word "Noritake" (or "Noritake" and "Japan"). Accordingly, Noritake marked pieces were shunned. To get a sense of the situation, consider the following hypothetical but yet quite realistic scenario. At an antique show, a Nippon collector from North America comes across a pair of seemingly identical, attractively decorated candlesticks. Both are in perfect condition and they are realistically priced as a pair. Candlesticks with just that motif have been on the collector's "wish list" for some time and the collector has never seen them for sale before. The collector is on the verge of purchasing them, but notices that one has the expected pre-1921 Nippon backstamp but the other one has a post-1921 Noritake backstamp. Given this, will the Nippon collector buy the pair?

Although I do not have any systematic survey data on the matter, many conversations with experienced North American collectors of and dealers in Nippon era porcelains convince me that many of them would choose not to purchase the Noritake marked item. Just as amazingly, I am convinced by similar conversations with North American "Noritake" collectors that they would make essentially the same decision. They would eschew the

Nippon marked piece. The only difference would be that, unlike their Nippon collecting brethren, they would not presume that the piece they refuse to buy was inferior in artistry or materials. In Japan or Great Britain, however, I believe most collectors would purchase the pair with little or no hesitation. Moreover I do not think they would believe that the different backstamps indicate that there must be a difference in the quality of the porcelain or the artistry of one or the other piece. Indeed, I suspect the questions posed for the North American buyers by our hypothetical scenario would mostly just seem strange to collectors in Japan and Great Britain. Old Noritake is Old Noritake. The essentially arbitrary North American 1921 boundary indicated by the shift in the words used in some (mostly European) backstamps simply has nothing to do with the desirability of a piece. Although Pat Murphy's splendid book is motivated by other, far more lofty goals, it pleases me that both the contents and spirit of Noritake for Europe will, per force, further mute is rather peculiar feature of the North American collecting scene.

Author's Note

David Spain is an acknowledged expert in Noritake porcelains and author of the influential "A to Z" Noritake books, also published by Schiffer. He also is editor of the "Noritake News," the newsletter of the Noritake Collector's Society, the much respected assembly of collectors and dealers which he was instrumental in founding.

I ntroduction

To write the first reference book dedicated solely to European export Noritake has been a challenge. Following the footsteps of such gifted and knowledgeable authors as Joan van Patten, David Spain, and the rest has been a daunting experience and I have leant heavily on the work that they have already completed in adding my own efforts to the seemingly endless task of reviewing and cataloguing the wares produced by the Noritake Company.

A small EPNS (Electro-Plated Nickel Silver) cake stand with two pretty and unusual plates was the first step in my journey. I noticed the little set at a small country antique fair in the English Midlands almost fifteen years ago, purchased it for £40 ($60), and, although I didn't recognize the backstamp at the time, was hooked by the quality of the decoration. I realized fairly quickly that there was, in fact, quite a lot of this Noritake stuff around, but no one was really buying the wares and, more importantly, no one seemed to know much about it.

Even then, in the early days, I realized that the quality was very good, and the range of pieces was incredible, so I set out to discover what I could about the company and the wares. I really drew a blank. None of the antique dealers that I talked to could tell me much, apart from the fact it was Japanese, which I had already figured out for myself as the backstamp read "Made in Japan" so I sought out a dealer in Japanese ceramics who told me that it was "cheap modern rubbish that nobody wanted."

Well, I wanted it and it certainly wasn't rubbish so I continued to search and in my local library I found a book by a Joan van Patten, "The Collector's Encyclopedia of Noritake." The book was a revelation to me, all the information and background and all the pictures were wonderful, and someone obviously knew about my new love. Then I read some more and realized that the book was American, and I had never seen anything like most of the pieces illustrated. The backstamp section started me thinking, and I checked carefully to discover that now I was really confused. The book was on Noritake porcelain from 1921 to 1941, but the blue backstamp on the seven or eight pieces I had already bought was registered in London in 1908. So, did this mean that my pieces were older than 1921? Why did the

book show about a hundred backstamps when I had been looking out for Noritake for some months and had only seen one? Where was all this wonderfully colorful Art Deco stuff, when everything I had seen was traditional in style and design? What had I stumbled across, and where could I find the answers?

Fourteen years later Noritake porcelain IS the family business. We have gone on from simple collecting to buying and selling the odd piece to becoming the biggest specialist dealers in Noritake and Noritake Nippon porcelain in the United Kingdom. In 2000, we founded the Noritake Collector's Club in Europe and the truth is we STILL don't know the answers to all the questions.

What we do know is that Noritake porcelain, for its sheer quality and diversity, rivals anything produced in Europe and America. Noritake is also one of an exclusive few companies that has been in continuous production of ceramic wares for over one hundred years.

Ichizaemon Morimura founded his company, Morimura Gumi, in 1876. Today the company is still producing wonderful porcelain, but has diversified into many areas, making that small Japanese export company into one of the world's largest commercial concerns.

This book has two objectives. Firstly, it is the first to catalogue, exclusively, Noritake's European export wares from the earliest days in 1891 until 1939. There are a number of excellent publications on Noritake, but all have been written and published in America and are dedicated, in the main, to the American export wares. As reference books, they are exceptional, however they, naturally, make very small mention of the large proportion of the output of the Noritake factory that came to Europe. The collectors and dealers in the United States have a different approach to Noritake which most English, European, and probably also Japanese collectors will find somewhat confusing. In the early days of the company, the Morimuras were faced with legislation regarding the marking of their export wares. This legislation differed between countries, and, consequently, export wares for different countries left the factory with different backstamps. This had no real effect on us in Europe as the export wares, with the exception of those early items bearing the plain Komaru mark, were marked with the words "Noritake" and/or "Japan." This has been common for all Noritake wares exported directly to Europe since the late 1890s. America, however, has gone down a completely different route.

As a result of the McKinley Tariff Act of 1891, all exports to America were marked "Nippon," until 1921 when the regulations changed, and after that everything was marked "Japan." From 1891 until 1921, the Noritake name, with very few exceptions, was not used in America, and the Noritake wares all carried "Nippon" backstamps. This changeover has created, in America, two different factions of collectors, two different collectors clubs, and, effectively, two different ranges of wares, both originating, in the main, from one factory. The collectors of "Nippon" are interested in ceramics from the country, Japan, and not necessarily wares made exclusively by Noritake, but the Noritake collectors' interests lie with wares with backstamps bearing the word "Noritake" which were therefore exported after 1921. Indeed, it was only after years of consultation and discussion that members of the International Nippon Collectors Club (INCC) agreed that certain wares bearing the Noritake mark were acceptable for their members to collect. The members of the Noritake Collectors Society (NCS) have no such problem, if it doesn't say "Noritake," then it's not collectible as Noritake.

This, of course, has a bearing on the many collectors in Great Britain and Europe. Until now, trying to research and identify European export Noritake has been difficult as the existing books are dedicated to either "Nippon" or "Noritake" with virtually no overlap. There has been, as a result of this division, a certain amount of conflicting information about the wares.

I hope that this book will go some way to redress the balance with some six hundred odd new pictures, and exclusive information about European Noritake. As far as we in Great Britain and Europe are concerned, there is no division. A large proportion of the wares illustrated can be compared to similar shapes and styles in both Nippon and Noritake books that are currently available so we can say that European export Noritake crosses that divide with impunity.

My second objective has been to make this a book for collectors of Noritake. By that I mean that I have tried to make the data easy to access, I have kept the background information to a minimum and tried to provide some ideas for new collectors and some guidelines for those with some experience. In my view, far too many antiques publications become platforms for the author to lecture in great detail on the subtle nuances of design and color, and discussion of early management politics within the company when what the collector needs to know are the answers to far simpler questions. What is it? What should it be worth? Is it rare? I hope this book will be able to answer some of those questions.

Finally, a thought about Noritake. To me, the most intriguing quality about the wares is that air of real mystery. The main Noritake factory was severely damaged during the Second World War and virtually all of the company records were lost so the information you see before you, in common with the information in all of the other works on Noritake and Noritake Nippon, has been the result of years of detective work, gleaning small snippets here and there, a lot of logical assumptions, and a degree of deduction and some minor guesswork. Enjoy!

Chapter One
A Man Called Morimura

The History of the Noritake Company

In 1876, in Tokyo, Ichizaemon Morimura founded a company called Morimura Gumi for the purpose of exporting Japanese made goods to America. The story, however, starts some twenty years earlier.

Japan had enjoyed an isolationist policy, strictly enforced by the ruling Shogunate for over 200 years. Since 1638, Japan had had virtually no contact with the outside world. Its citizens were banned from traveling abroad and visitors were totally unwelcome, even unfortunate sailors, shipwrecked on Japan's shores were dealt with very harshly, a pitiful few surviving to tell the tale. At this time in history, America was the New World, barely settled with the intrepid colonists trying to find a way to coexist with the Native American Indians. Spain and England were still ravaging South and Central America, and each other on a regular basis, but some adventurers were finding their way to the Orient. The Shogunate of the time viewed Western influence as a threat to their advanced and orderly, although sometimes barbaric, society and simply barred all intercourse and communication with all and any representatives of Western civilization. There were few exceptions to this rule although a limited number of Dutch and Chinese merchants were allowed limited access to the country through the port of Nagasaki and the Shogun tolerated Jesuit missionaries on a strictly controlled basis.

In 1853, therefore, it was an isolated and insular Japan that viewed, with some trepidation, the small American squadron, commanded by Commodore Matthew C. Perry, enter Japanese waters and drop anchor in Yedo (to be renamed Tokyo) Bay. Commodore Perry was eventually received by the Shogun and he presented a letter from the President of the United States at that time, Millard Fillmore. President Fillmore, soon to leave office, asked for a simple agreement between the United States and Japan to set up a basic trade agreement, port facilities to receive American ships to allow them to reprovision and make repairs, and a guarantee of safety and repatriation for shipwrecked American mariners.

This simple agreement met with cautious approval from the current Shogun, who, more enlightened than his predecessors, agreed to take the diplomatic process to the next stage. Commodore Perry returned to America with the encouraging news, and President Fillmore's successor, President Pierce, who was also keen to open trade links with Japan, sent Commodore Perry back to Japan with the outline of a formal agreement.

Commodore Perry arrived back in Japan in February 1854, dropping anchor off the port of Kanagawa in the 25th of the month. Things then moved quickly, and on 31st February 1854 the Treaty of Kanagawa (later renamed Yokohama) was signed by Commodore Perry and the Shogun. This treaty complied in principal with the outlines of President Fillmore's original letter, and, in addition, allowed for the establishment of formal diplomatic relations between the two countries. There was to be an American Consulate in the port of Shimoda, and this port, along with the port of Hakodate, was to be opened to foreign trade. Commodore Perry returned to the United States with the treaty, which was ratified in the American legislature in 1855. Later that year, the first American Consul, Townsend Harris returned to Japan and took up residence in the new American Consulate in Shimoda.

By 1860, trade with America was growing, and the Japanese, at least those living and working in and around the ports of Shimoda and Hakodate, were becoming used to the sight of Western traders and sailors in the streets of their cities. The Tokugawa Shogunate decided it was high time to send their own diplomatic mission to the United States, and an envoy was chosen to leave for America. A young man in the Japanese diplomatic service, one Ichizaemon Morimura, was tasked to buy gifts and foreign currency for the diplomatic mission, and noted the huge disparity in exchange rates which greatly favored the Americans. He soon became concerned that the increasing unilateral trade environment, currently not of great proportions, but destined to grow as demand especially among the Japanese ruling classes rose, could affect the Japanese economy. Japan, having been isolated for many years, had no real international trading acumen, and Morimura foresaw that this trade could actually topple the Japanese economy, leaving them reliant on American trade to support their own country financially. He consulted with his great friend and mentor, Professor Fukuzawa, who had a simple answer to the problem. Start a Japanese export industry to bring the money back into Japan.

In 1866, Japan at last lifted the ban on traveling abroad for the purposes of education and trade. Until this point, it was actually illegal in Japan to build a boat with ocean going capability, and the only shipping Japan owned were coastal traders and fishing vessels. In the same year, Ichizaemon sent his younger brother, Yutaka (Toyo) to study under his old friend, Professor Fukuzawa, where he learnt about trade and business and studied English. Ichizaemon spent the next few years learning all he could about the West and the potential for setting up his own trading company. His diplomatic connections served him well, and by the time he founded Morimura Gumi with his brother in 1876, he was ready to embark on a career in the export trade.

Toyo left Japan that same year aboard the United States ship "Oceanic." He was 23 years old, almost the same age as his older brother when Ichizaemon had first discussed the possibilities of an export company with Professor Fukuzawa. In September 1876, Toyo opened their first retail shop, in Front Street in the city of New York. A year later, Toyo started his own company in America, Hinode Shokai, but this partnership was short-lived and in the following year, 1878, Morimura Bros. Co. was registered in New York. Toyo now had the company running well in New York, and expanded to include a wholesale business as well as retail outlets.

The company started with the import of a wide range of goods including Japanese general antiques, Laquerwork items, wooden and bamboo furniture, and some ceramic items, mainly decorative pieces and some traditional Japanese tea-wares. By 1882, Toyo, proving to be an astute businessman, had identified that the most profitable market was ceramics. There was a growing demand for Japanese ceramic wares and his trade in vases, tea-wares and fancies was growing rapidly. Ichizaemon, back in Japan, was quickly taking up contracts to supply the wares to meet Toyo's requirements, mainly purchasing porcelain bodies from several factories in the Aichi region for decoration in one of the several painting and decorating factories the company now owned within the Greater Tokyo area. This region produced a porcelain with a grayish appearance, which was soon to cause the company problems.

The following year, in 1883, Toyo made a decision that was to prove momentous for Morimura Gumi. He purchased a simple French manufactured porcelain teacup, and shipped it back to his brother in Japan, indicating that demand for this style of wares was rising rapidly, and asking if Ichizaemon would look into the possibilities of producing wares of similar shape and style. This single small cup caused a major furor within Morimura Gumi. It had a handle, completely at odds with the traditional Japanese tea bowl that had not, and the body was pure white hard paste porcelain. All of the porcelain bodies produced in Japan at that time were of a grayish white color, and the research and development needed to reproduce this body was to occupy the company for the next twenty years. Ichizaemon immediately set out to reproduce the shape and style of European dinnerwares. This was the first indication of the way the company was to go in its growth and development, following Western trends and reproducing its own versions of popular ceramics for the Western market.

By 1884, the company owned various sites around the Tokyo area, mainly painting and decorating facilities, including larger plants at Kyoto and Nagoya. Efficiency was becoming a problem with so many different operations, and there was also a growing need to manufacture the porcelain bodies in house and also gear up with research, development, and design. The Morimura Company planned a massive expansion program that was going to take almost twenty years to complete. Ichizaemon decided that he would move all the operations under one roof, and this expansion, along with land acquisition and building works amalgamated all the existing facilities on to one site. Meanwhile, the search for the elusive pure white body continued, and, in 1889, Ichizaemon visited the Paris World Fair, combining this trip with visits to many porcelain producing centers in Europe and Britain. He found that his reception in Britain was decidedly cool, but did discover that his production methods and the technology he was employing was far behind that used by the European factories. He immediately embarked on a comprehensive modernization program to bring his factory up to that standard with new kilns and up to date technology.

Morimura's visit to Europe brought other changes. Although he was not made particularly welcome in Staffordshire, other European countries were not as distant, and Ichizaemon began a relationship with Rosenfeld, one of the smaller European manufacturers. Rosenfeld was also a family business, based in Carlsbad, Austria, and, in 1902, members of the Rosenfeld family visited New York and Japan to discuss an exchange of technology. Rosenfeld was to help with producing a white porcelain body, and, in return, were to receive help to develop their gilding techniques. As a result of this exchange, and with additional help and advice of a German ceramics technologist, Dr. Hecht of the Seger Institute, the company produced its first pure white porcelain body.

In 1904, the company, still Morimura Gumi, was to change the structure of the business and form a new holding company. This company, Nippon Tokei Gomei Kaisha, brought all the various parts of the company together under a central management umbrella, and this central management facility was to be installed on the site of the new company headquarters. This was to be situated in a brand new factory on the outskirts of a little village near Nagoya called Noritake. This area, named after the old feudal landowners — descendants of the ancient Noritake clan, was to become the biggest ceramics manufacturing area in Japan. The village's name would be used as the company's trademark, making it one of the most well known and respected names in the world ceramics industry.

Having now been able to produce a pure white porcelain body, the company continued development work on the other major problem that had dogged their efforts for many years. In spite of major sustained effort, the company were unable to produce a satisfactory dinner plate. The basic shape was alien to the Japanese who had never employed the European style wide flat plate, and the company turned once again to their friends at Rosenfeld. They also asked for advice from the Seger Institute. Dr. Kramer of Seger, who analyzed and modified the porcelain clay mix, and also made some modifications to the actual dimensions of the plate bases, finally solved the problems. In July 1913, Nippon Tokei successfully produced their first eight and ten inch dinner plates in white porcelain. A year later, in June of 1914, the company produced their first 93 piece white porcelain dinner service.

Nippon Tokei were able, subsequently, to quickly establish a good overseas market for European style dinnerwares that grew very rapidly. America, by virtue of its sheer size, was mainly rural and a number of new companies were marketing their goods via mail order catalogues or through teams of traveling salesmen who toured the country areas selling their wares using samples and catalogues. As incentives to buy their mainstream products, a number of these companies offered free bonus gifts or "premiums."

Several of these companies offered Nippon Tokei wares as premiums. Two of the major players, the Jewel Tea Company and the Larkin Company, became instrumental in popularizing Noritake wares across America. Nippon Tokei would produce a number of patterns and styles exclusively for these companies, so some very popular and collectible patterns actually started life as premiums. Among the most notable are Azalea and Tree in the Meadow, which have found their way to Europe, and although Azalea, with the American export backstamp, is quite rare, versions of Tree in the Meadow are quite common, and can be found with the European backstamp.

Nippon Tokei continued, throughout the first twenty years of the twentieth century, to produce high quality dinnerwares and fancies. The company, following its success in America, ventured into Europe, with the help of Rosenfeld. The company registered the Komaru mark in London in 1908, which was the first year that Noritake appeared as a trade mark within a company backstamp, and started to import high quality fancies, followed by dinnerwares from 1914. For the first time, the company, which had concentrated very much on export business, turned to their own domestic market, producing Japanese style dinnerwares for home sales. Although the first domestic backstamp bearing the legend "Noritake" was registered, according to the company records, in 1908, the first domestic production using this backstamp did not leave the factory until 1930.

Morimura, ever the businessman was always looking for innovation and new markets to address. Market research showed that although the American market in the late 1920s and early 1930s was showing huge potential for the new shapes, colors, and luster glazes of Art Deco style, there was still a demand for more traditional wares in Europe. Although mainland Europe was very much in favor of the glassy hard paste porcelain, there was a growing market in Britain for soft paste porcelain, popularly known as Bone China. The aftermath of the Great Depression of 1929 had caused a global drop in international trade, and the company was anxious to attack any available market for their wares.

In 1933, Nippon Tokei exported the first bone china wares to Britain, and also into India and Southeast Asia (under the Royal Crockery (RC) trademark). These bone china wares proved very successful and popular as traditional style, high quality dinnerwares, and they did very well in Britain, matching the style and quality of the Staffordshire factories at a lower price. As a result, the main factory at Nagoya was expanded with the addition of more kilns devoted to production of the new bone china wares. These kilns, with six chimneys, each standing over one hundred and fifty feet high became part of the city skyline after completion in 1938, until their eventual demolition in 1979. At the height of their production, the company employed over 4000 painters and decorators in their decorating shops, producing hand painted and hand finished wares for export to America and Europe as well as the domestic market. The total output of the factory during the 1930s was greater than the combined output of all of the main Staffordshire factories over the same period.

The advent of the Second World War had a disastrous effect on Nippon Tokei, with the factory all but ceasing production of ceramics for the duration, turning their efforts instead to the production of abrasives and grinding wheels, an activity which was to continue after the end of the war as a new direction for the company. The main factory was very badly damaged towards the end of the war, and the majority of the skilled workforce was lost, either in active service or as a result of the bombing. Ceramic production recommenced very soon after the cessation of hostilities; however, the absence of the old skills was apparent, and the company—realizing that production was not of pre-war quality—used a different backstamp, "Rose China," as an interim measure. The United States, whose marketplace had been instrumental in the growth of the company, was significant in the company's resurrection in the late 1940s. Major contracts with the American Eighth Army and the Military Government for supply of utility wares provided the cashflow and turnover that Nippon Tokei needed to get back into production, and to rebuild and replace the plant and machinery. It took some time, but the major problem was replacing key staff and tradesmen, retraining the new labor force in the old skills to improve the quality of the output. By 1948, the company was happy that the quality of the wares was nearing the old pre-war level, and re-introduced the Noritake trademark.

Once the company threw off the majority of the long term effects of the war, and production came back up to approach pre-war levels, Nippon Tokei, once again, looked at the marketplace and the potential for new products. During their research into the production of bone china in the early 1930s, they had gained a lot of knowledge of the chemical and physical effects of various porcelain mixes, producing, in 1935, a completely new type of porcelain. Production costs of this new material were higher, and due to price constraints within the worldwide ceramics market, the project was shelved at the time as being financially unfeasible to put into major production. In the early 1950s the project was re-evaluated, and the features of the new porcelain were examined in detail. It would not deform during firing, a common problem with porcelain, would take better coloring and a richer glaze, all at a lower firing temperature than normal porcelains. The company made a decision to market the new porcelain as "Fine China" and started production for export and domestic use in 1953. Fine China arrived in the UK in the late 1950s and proved an instant success in good quality, medium priced dinnerwares.

The Company's research and development program has continued since then with new products and materials. Ivory China, which was hard paste porcelain with an ivory glaze, was introduced in 1959. This body was so popular that Noritake Imari still produces wares from the same original formula. In 1963, a new factory was built at Miyoshi to specialize in production of export wares, mainly for the American market, which continues in production today. A year later, in 1964, the company released a new range of heat resistant reinforced porcelain, which they called "Progression China." Initially this was destined solely for the American market, but Progression China has now been patented worldwide. Demand for this new product resulted in the construction of another new facility, at Kyushu, which was dedicated to production of a wide range of Progression Chinawares. Stoneware was the next step in diversification into new areas, and another plant was dedicated to the production of stone china at Tajimi. This also is still in production under the Noritake Nichiyoo banner.

The year 1972 saw the introduction of Noritake earthenwares. The company had been manufacturing earthenware, in a limited capacity, since the mid-1930s; but, demand for earthenware tablewares was increasing and the company launched Craftone in that year, followed by several other brand names including the popular Keltcraft ranges. The company also started major production of earthenware sanitary goods at this time.

Overseas production of Noritake wares started in the early 1970s with plants opened in Sri Lanka in 1972, and the Philippines in 1973. Of interest is the acquisition, in 1975, of the ailing Arklow Pottery in Ireland. The Arklow Pottery had the facilities and infrastructure in place, but needed the cash injection provided by Noritake to update their machinery and production line. Some of Noritake's existing product lines were introduced, with small adaptations, such as Noritake Keltcraft, and also new products such as Misty Isle Collection were introduced. This overseas manufacturing and distribution policy has now resulted in Noritake or a Noritake subsidiary having a presence in almost every country in the world.

Product diversification has been very successful for the Noritake Company. The enforced move into abrasives in 1939 has been followed by sanitary wares, as we have mentioned, and also spark plugs and auto electrical components (NGK is a Noritake company). The firm also produces high quality crystal and glassware, melamine, very high quality stainless steel, electronic components, and diamond cutting tools.

It is worth a small, final mention that the company we all know as Noritake didn't actually change its Japanese name officially to The Noritake Company Ltd. until 1981.

Chapter Two
The European Export Backstamps

The Noritake Company records are notoriously incomplete regarding backstamps, but the total number of recorded backstamps is in excess of 300. This total includes both export backstamps and those for domestic use within Japan and also variations of wording and color, but is still a large number to consider.

Fortunately, we are concerned specifically with the backstamps that appeared on Noritake European export pieces from 1891 until 1939, although there are one or two exceptions that we will discuss. To clarify the exact nature of these backstamps, real illustrations from actual pieces will be used so that you see them "in the flesh," rather than in a representation.

pear in Europe, probably in the late 1890s. Noritake recognizes this as possible as, although this mark was registered in Japan in 1906, it could have been used earlier. Although it is a stylized symbol, it does contain elements of the Morimura family crest.

The Noritake Blue mark. First registered 1908.

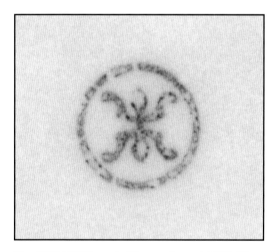

The KOMARU mark. First registered 1908. Blue.

The Noritake Green mark. First registered 1908.

This KOMARU symbol forms the base of a large number of backstamps used by the company, and the base of all the early European backstamps. This symbol is a fusion of Japanese calligraphic symbols, which tells a story. It represents the difficulties that the Japanese people faced when dealing with foreign cultures and customs coupled with a pair of spears to represent the ways to break through the cultural barrier, and all surrounded by a circle to represent a harmonious solution. The backstamp, found in the blue illustrated here was registered in London in 1908; however, it appears regularly on Moriagewares and other pieces which suggests that, in fact, it was the first Noritake backstamp to ap-

The Noritake Red mark. First registered 1908.

The three marks illustrated here are actually three colorways of the commonest Noritake mark found in Europe. There is also a variation of the blue color which would strictly make four colorways in this mark; however, there is no evidence to suggest that this variation signifies any difference in the wares. All these marks were registered in London in 1908. There are a number of variations to this basic mark which may have some significance in the fact that the Green and Red versions of this mark were re-registered in London in 1949.

Some collectors have formed the opinion that the different colors denote different qualities, which is a misconception which probably stems from one of the early Noritake Nippon marks. The Maple Leaf mark, illustrated in Chapter Three, was used in both blue and green for Europe, and the company is certain that green was used on first quality wares and blue on second quality wares, but this is not the case with the Noritake Komaru marks. All three marks were first registered at the same time, and there is no difference in quality denoted by the different colors.

Accurate dating from these marks is not really possible. The Noritake Company readily accept that their own records are incomplete and although they are certain about registration dates of their export marks, this is probably because they have been able to confirm those dates with the various foreign registration authorities. The company cannot, however, say with any real accuracy when specific marks were brought into use, when they were discontinued, and, unfortunately, Noritake never used year ciphers or marks on their wares. In many ways this is a sad lack of foresight; however, the company, in the early days, would have no inkling of how popular and collectible their wares would become. The only real clues that we have are that the plain Komaru has never been seen in any of the later styles and patterns, which would indicate a cessation of use of that mark when the three standard marks were registered, and that the blue mark was not re-registered in 1949 along with the green and red, which would seem to indicate that the blue mark was not used after 1939.

The only guide we have, therefore, is related to the style of decoration and the mold shapes of the pieces. This holds true especially for the highly decorated pieces in classical style which we can match in terms of style, patterns, and mold shape with American Export pieces carrying Nippon backstamps. We know that the Nippon backstamps were not used after 1921, as a result of the change in American import legislation, so that would indicate that these pieces were, in the main, produced before 1921.

What we can say with certainty, as evidence that the three Komaru colors were used concurrently, is that the Desert Scene pattern (which is probably the most popular pattern for collectors) can bear a backstamp in any of the three colors. However the style and pattern indicate that the Desert Scene would have been popular, and therefore in main production, probably from around 1918. There is also illustrated in this book a second variation, the "Matte" finish, in which the gilding is of a different style with definite "Art Deco" elements, which we can infer was an updated version following the Egyptianesque fashion which came into massive popularity following Howard Carter's discovery of the tomb of the Pharoah Tut-ankh-Amen in 1922. Examples of Desert Scene, in the European style, are also illustrated in Joan Van Patten's Nippon books, carrying Nippon backstamps which would date them before 1921, so this pattern obviously spanned the American Nippon/Noritake changeover period, but would not have been popular after the late 1920s when style became far more simplistic. So, we have an early pattern, which is of top quality, bearing either Blue, Green, or Red Komaru marks, which is proof evident that the three Komaru backstamps were registered at the same time and used concurrently throughout the period 1908 until 1939.

In conclusion, then, it comes down to experience to date Noritake with any accuracy; but, a VERY basic rule of thumb is this: The better quality and more "traditional" the decoration and gilding, the older the piece is likely to be.

Finally, there are some variations of which the collector must be aware. As this book is essentially dedicated to Noritake produced between the late 1890s and the beginning of World War Two (1897 to 1939), the backstamps for that period are those we have discussed. However, in addition to the re-issue of the Green and Red marks in 1949, Noritake, in 1951, also registered a variation of the standard Komaru mark, in two colors, Green and Gold, with the wording changed under the Komaru symbol from "Made in Japan" to "Import." A variation on these two marks was registered, again, in Green or Gold, in 1954, with the word "Foreign" in place of "Made in Japan." So, while the standard Green and Red marks could be either Pre- or Post-war, although style and quality would normally be the differentiator, the later Green and Gold marks with Foreign or Import are certainly Post-war, and not covered by the scope of this book. It is important to mention these later marks, however, as it is easy for them to be mistaken for earlier backstamps.

Chapter Three
The Nippon Connection

The Noritake Company and the Nippon Backstamp

There has always been a certain amount of controversy over wares bearing a backstamp that consists of, or includes, the word "NIPPON."

Nippon is not a manufacturer, or a factory, but simply the Japanese word for Japan, in Roman script. Nippon first appeared on Japanese export wares as a result of the passing of the McKinley Tariff Act in October 1890 in the United States. This Act came into being sponsored by William McKinley, a Republican congressman, as a result of the fears of a number of American manufacturers who wanted some form of protection from imported goods taking a significant share of the American domestic retail market. These businessmen felt that, were the American public able to discriminate, then they would favor domestic manufactured goods, rather than imported goods.

The Act became law on 1st March 1891, and the essence of this legislation made compulsory the clear marking of all imported goods with the country of origin. This applied to all imported goods, not just ceramics, and imports from all countries. The Japanese exporters, Morimura included, were obliged to comply, so all Japanese exports to the United States were marked Nippon in some form. This practice continued until March 1921, when the American government decided that, as Nippon was an Anglicized version of a Japanese word, and the letter of the law called for goods to be marked with the country of origin "in English," and the "proper" English word was actually "Japan," that goods should now be marked Japan instead of Nippon.

All very simple and logical stuff, but it does give us a "dating" window for Nippon marked wares. To comply with this legislation, therefore, we can safely say that all Nippon marked wares, with the small number of pieces that overlapped the various dates by a small margin, should be dated between 1891 and 1921.

It should be made clear at this point that not all ceramics marked Nippon were made by Noritake. It is certain that a large proportion of these wares were, in fact, manufactured by the company, some authorities

on the subject put the figure as high as 90%, however, that is not a firm percentage. Generally, the Nippon backstamps generated by Noritake are well documented in the very good range of Nippon reference books by Joan van Patten, and in most cases, Noritake wares stand out simply by their style and quality from other manufacturers of the time.

The style of the Nippon marked Noritake export wares is, in general, highly decorative with complex regular shapes, heavy gilding, enameling, beading, and hand painting, in the style of the best of the British and European factories of that era. In the late nineteenth century, Britain was the most powerful country in the world in terms of political and social influence, and British taste was very much reflected in the export wares produced during this period. William Morris' Aesthetic Movement had given way to the late Victorian Art Nouveau period, characterized by heavy decoration, sinuous lines, and liberal use of plant and animal elements. This style was in demand. Japanese manufacturers who were now producing wares specifically destined for the West, met that demand. Cups were of several different styles but had handles (previously unused in Japan where the tradition was for handleless tea bowls) and plates were produced with rims instead of the traditional Japanese flat centers. Vases were produced in pairs, usually with "mirrored" decoration instead of as single examples, and many items were produced complementary to Western table manners and habits, such as condensed milk containers and smoker's sets. Thus, the wares produced and exported from Japan during the Nippon era, carrying various forms of the Nippon backstamp, were influenced by British style, but destined, in the main, for the American market.

It is interesting to note that although the styles, certainly up until around 1910 at least, were very much to the European taste, none of these wares were exported directly into Europe. A study of the known Noritake backstamps of the period shows up some interesting facts that lead us to some even more interesting conclusions.

We know, from the history of the company, that the Morimura concern was exporting from around 1876, and their wares fell, until 1921 at least, into the Nippon period. We can, with certainty, identify a number of backstamps used by the company during the period, that incorporate the word Nippon. Some of the more common versions are illustrated here.

The "Maple Leaf" mark, registered in Japan, 1908; however, pieces bearing this backstamp have been dated as early as 1891, the year that the design was submitted for patent approval, making this one of the first Noritake marks to comply with the McKinley legislation. The colors may be green, blue, or red. The Noritake Company tells us that the green was used on first quality items, and the blue and red marks on second quality. Pieces bearing the green and blue marks may be found in Europe.

The "Rising Sun" mark is another early version, registered in 1911 in Japan. This mark can be found in Europe in Blue.

These were the only early Noritake "Nippon" backstamps that were directly imported into Europe before the European export backstamps were officially registered. Wares marked with other "Nippon" backstamps have found their way into Europe, and the following are "Nippon" backstamps that we can say with certainty originated in the Noritake factory. These are all "export" backstamps and were all used on wares destined for the American market.

The "Komaru," which is associated with the Noritake Company, in combination with Nippon. Registered in 1908 in Japan.

This backstamp, registered in 1911, is the first mark to bear the legend "RC" for Royal Crockery. This mark was printed in blue and green.

This backstamp was also registered in 1911, and can be found with the "hand painted" in red and the remainder in green.

The first of the Noritake "M in a Wreath" backstamps was also registered in 1911. The wreath is actually the Morimura family crest, printed upside down. The wreath symbolizes hanging wisteria, and the "M" is, of course, for the Morimura family.

This backstamp incorporated a stylized Komaru symbol, and was another registered in 1911.

A combination of symbols and wording made up this backstamp. Also registered in 1911, the NipponToki was a partial company name, having become Nippon Tokei Gomei Kaisha in 1904, and Nagoya was the region in which the head office was situated.

This, the last of the 1911 backstamps was simple, with just the two words. Found in green or a light pinkie red, the mark was also used domestically for undecorated pieces.

An alternate version of the previous backstamp used the company trademark "Noritake" instead of the company name. As Nippon was now missing, it replaced Nagoya on the base.

This backstamp, registered in 1912, was destined for American exports, but has been seen, in blue, in Europe.

This backstamp, also registered in 1912 also contains the two key words, Noritake and Nippon. It was used in green and maroon, and was for American export.

Study of a number of the very good publications, references, and books dedicated to Nippon ceramic wares of the period confirms that over 80% of the export pieces identified and illustrated bear one of these twelve backstamps, so we can be confident that the vast majority of the wares produced and exported during this period originated in one of the Morimura's factories.

There is, however, no record of any Noritake backstamp registered in the United Kingdom during that period bearing the word Nippon, nor, interestingly enough, were any backstamps registered in America bearing the word "Noritake." The early English backstamps, all registered in 1908, have the Komaru symbol, Noritake, or Made in Japan either as single elements or combinations of these three elements. The registration date, 1908, is clearly in the middle of the Nippon period so it would appear that Nippon Tokei Gomei Kaisha, as the Noritake company was then known, had made a specific decision to export to Europe only under the Noritake trademark, reserving the Nippon backstamp for their American export wares.

This seems a very interesting proposition. Had the company a specific reason for doing this, or was it simply oversight?

Further study reveals that over 40% of the pieces illustrated in this book, dedicated to European Export Noritake, are identical in mold shape, pattern, or both to pieces carrying Nippon backstamps and exported to America.

A typical example would be the scenic coffee can and saucer illustrated below left. This coffee can and saucer is almost identical in shape and pattern to the coffee can and saucer illustrated below right. If, however, we look at the backstamp, we can see that it is the Nippon "M in a Wreath mark" which is an American Export mark.

Underside of coffee can showing Nippon mark.

Scenic coffee can and saucer.

Scenic coffee can and saucer.

We can see from this that the Noritake company was exporting identical wares to the two major areas under two different sets of backstamps, using, in the main, the Noritake banner for Europe and the Nippon banner for America. This was certainly not an attempt to keep the two markets separate as a small percentage for these shapes and patterns, notably scenic wares such as "Desert Scene," certainly went to America with Noritake "M in a Wreath" backstamps.

The answer to this probably is that the company was superb at marketing, and, more importantly, reading market trends. We know that in the early days of the company's export activities, style was dictated by Great Britain and Europe and the export wares were very European in style. It would, therefore, be logical to expect wares in the European style to be popular in America and to see those wares exported to both markets. As America started to develop its own style, the popularity of the European influence started to wane, and the company began to produce wares specifically for America. This is ably illustrated when we look at the Art Deco influence on ceramics. Although the basic tenets of the Art Deco style remained the same, the taste differed across the Atlantic. Lusterwares are a typical area to look at: in Europe, luster glazes became popular, but not to the same extent as in America, so much of the later Noritake which came to Europe, while Art Deco in style, maintained classical glazes and finishes. The American wares of the period, however, demonstrated the ability of the company to produce fabulous colors, shapes, and designs in luster glazes which were never exported to Europe but were immensely popular in America.

So, the two biggest export markets grew apart, but we must also consider the way that the company's products were actually marketed and sold in the two areas. The American market and the growing popularity of Noritake in America sprang from the initial introduction of the wares in quantity to the region via the traveling salesman's "premiums." Effectively, the wares were given away for many years as free gifts, so, as long as the quality was good, there was no great need for direct product identification and a brand name marketing campaign as the wares gained in popularity almost automatically.

There was no such market in Europe, however, and the wares were competing directly against the big names in British and European ceramics. There had to be a direct marketing effort and immediate brand name identification. As the backstamp is the simplest way to identify a particular manufacturer, the company started with the Noritake Komaru mark, and used it exclusively until well after the Second World War, even re-registering the green and red marks in 1949. The differences in import identification legislation between the United States and Europe made it possible to market in this way and the Rosenfeld Company who, having been of technical assistance to the company in the early days around the turn of the century, was now prime importer and wholesaler of Noritake wares in Europe. They marketed the wares under the Noritake brand name as quality porcelain at very competitive prices and were able to open up a market for the product, initially through their own London showrooms, and then through a number of quality stores in the capital and the provinces. Their marketing strategy was based on quality at a "good" price, and their target market was not so much the "upper classes" but rather those who had made their money through "trade," businessmen and merchants who wanted the quality, but did not want to pay the price of top quality British and European wares. This was extremely successful, but led very much to the growing rift in style between the European and American markets. The purchasers of Noritake in Britain and Europe were in the market for traditional quality and design, and were very wary of avante garde styles and patterns, thus the market for innovative wares did not grow to anything like the market in America, which was thirsty for innovation and modern style.

So, we can see that the two differing marketing strategies and differences in import legislation led to this division in exports. In effect, the company started with a single range of styles, designs, and mold shapes, exported simply under the Nippon and Noritake backstamps to Europe and America respectively, but as style evolved, ended with two different markets for their wares. The disparity in backstamps was therefore probably a simple result of this marketing policy, rather than a direct effort to separate the two markets.

This simple difference in uniformity of backstamps has caused an interesting and long term effect within the collecting community of America. We, in Britain and Europe, have seen continuous import of Noritake marked wares from around 1897 right through the period covered by this book until 1939 with virtual uniformity of backstamp identification, so consider the wares to be a single collectible medium. In America, however, there is a definite split at the 1921 point when Nippon "became" Noritake. There are "Nippon" collectors and "Noritake" collectors, and very little overlap; indeed, it would seem unlikely that a Nippon collector would even consider adding a Noritake piece to the collection and vice versa, even though the two differently marked wares surely originated in the same factory. Perhaps, life is simpler in Europe!

Chapter Four

The Evolution of Noritake Porcelain

Design and Style Influences 1890 to 1939

The period which we consider to be the "Golden Era" for Noritake porcelain runs from around 1890 until the beginning of the second World War. During this period, the company produced what is probably their best work in terms of quality and diversity. At the height of their renown the company employed 4000 painters alone, producing hand painted pieces with expertise that rivaled the best of the European factories, and their gilding skills were probably the best in the world. The company's major strength, however, was certainly in their ability to read and match market trends and produce work that was consistently evolving as styles and fashions changed over the period. Noritake's wares always mirrored the "current" fashion. The firm was always extremely efficient and flexible enough to modify prevailing designs or produce new patterns and shapes to take advantage of new or innovative trends in style.

Noritake tended not to be innovative themselves, preferring, wisely in retrospect, to be very quick to produce a version of a latest style that conformed to the essence of that fashion, but had Noritake's trademark quality and unique individuality. It is wrong to say that the company simply copied European pieces, but they certainly were able to capture the spirit of the particular European style without reproducing exact imitations. This unique ability kept the company at the forefront of the ceramics market, where they would have stayed, were it not for the ravages of the war.

For us to consider how this evolution came about, we must look further afield than simply the ceramics market. This fifty year period saw the biggest and most radical changes in world-wide culture and lifestyle in history, driven by a huge number of events and developments that had a fundamental impact across the globe. The world changed more in these fifty years than in any comparable fifty years that had gone before, and events became really global for the first time.

In order to fully understand these changes, we must look at a number of the most important of these events, and some from the fifty years before, from 1840 and evaluate their influence on the world at large.

1837
Queen Victoria becomes Queen of England.
I.K.Brunel completes the first Transatlantic steamer, the "Great Western."
Wheatstone & Cooke, a pair of British electrical engineers patent the Telegraph.

1838
The first scheduled steamship route from England to America is established.

1839
Dageurre, in France, and Talbot in England demonstrate photography for the first time.

1842
The Chinese opium wars finally end following the Treaty of Nanking. Chinese ports are opened to international trade.

1844
Samuel Morse demonstrates telegraphic communications in America with a message sent from Baltimore to Washington.

1845
The "Free Trade" legislation, introduced into English law by Robert Peel opens up trade between Britain, Europe, and America by doing away with all export duties and most import duties.

1846
The Irish Potato Famine results in a huge increase in Irish emigration to America.

1849
John Ruskin publishes a treatise, "The Seven Lamps of Architecture," which popularizes the Gothic style, and England sees a "Gothic Revival" in style and fashion.

1851
The Great Exhibition was held in the Crystal Palace in London. This was the first true World Fair, and the Crystal Palace was purpose-built to house it.
The American Isaac Singer invents the sewing machine.

1852

Although the Montgolfier brothers had demonstrated ballooning with a tethered hot air balloon almost seventy years before in November 1783, the first true airship flight was undertaken by the Frenchman Henri Giffard.

1853

Commodore Perry travels to Japan with a diplomatic approach from the United States.

1855

The Paris World Exhibition opens. This is to be the first of a long series of exhibitions that will contribute significantly to the evolution of style over the next decades. Townsend Harris is appointed first American Consul to Japan. Trade between America and Japan commences.

1857

The first Transatlantic Telegraph cable is laid. Full instantaneous two-way communication is now possible between England and America.

1860

Etienne Lenoir, a French engineer, invents the internal combustion engine. First Japanese diplomatic mission to America.

1861

William Morris establishes an association of applied arts craftsmen, whose aim is reformation in the applied arts, especially Gothic Revival.

1863

London opens the first underground railway. This achievement, and the innovations in civil engineering that were perfected to make this project a reality, became the template for similar projects in Europe and America.

1875

The Larkin Company was founded in Buffalo, New York.

1876

Alexander Graham Bell, a Scots expatriate, invents the telephone in America. Another American, Thomas Edison, invents the phonograph, while, in Germany, Karl Benz builds a motorized tricycle, the forerunner of the internal combustion engined car. Back in America, Philadelphia stages its Centennial Exhibition which features a Renaissance revival. Ichizaemon Morimura founds Morimura Gumi in Japan, and his brother Toyo travels to New York.

1880

The Arts and Crafts Movement begins in England. This movement, bored with the retrospective Gothic Revival, advocated a return to simplistic and clean designs, executed by hand using natural materials and, although this movement's popularity was comparatively short lived in Europe, being all but finished with twenty years, the Movement would be adopted in America around ten years later, and would continue there until around 1915.

1885

Karl Benz shows the first true car, while Gottleib Daimler patents a petrol engine for a motorcycle.

1887

Heinrich Hertz, a German physicist, demonstrates the transmission of radio waves.

1888

Kodak develops a popular, easy to use camera system, and photography becomes a tool of the masses, rather than a specialized, scientific craft.

1889

The Paris Universal exhibition shows the potential of electric power for the first time. Ichizaemon Morimura, by now a well established ceramics manufacturer and exporter, visits to discover how outdated his Japanese production facilities are in comparison with Europe.

1890

The Arts and Craft Movement gains popularity in America, where the Chicago World Fair shows, for the first time, many American designs and innovations in style. Oscar Wilde begins his "Aesthetic Movement." This movement, which saw art as beauty, was strongly influenced by Japanese style. William Morris, of Gothic Revival fame, quickly embraced the new ideas, and his company, seen as the epitome of good taste, quickly became the leading retailer of furnishings in the Aesthetic style. The Aesthetic Movement led to what would develop into "Art Nouveau," although the actual term would not be used until much later.

1895

Guglielmo Marconi, an Italian physicist, invents the wireless. The Lumiere brothers show the first film and Samuel Bing opens his shop, "La Maison de l'Art Nouveau"(House of New Art). His shop and gallery become the showpiece for French and International Art Nouveau designs and the phrase "Art Nouveau" was born.

1896

Charles Rennie Mackintosh founds the Glasgow School of Arts.

1898

Zeppelin invents the airship.

1899

The headquarters of the Austrian Art Nouveau movement becomes based in Joseph Olbrich's Secessionist Art Gallery in Vienna. The Austrian movement influences Secessionist styles, some adopted by British ceramics studios and manufacturers, including Minton.

1900

The Paris Universal Exhibition becomes a showcase for Art Nouveau style and design.

1901

Queen Victoria is succeeded by Edward VII. Marconi sends the first successful Transatlantic radio transmissions and Frank Lloyd Wright comes to prominence following the publication of his lecture, "The Art and Craft of the Machine."

1902

Carlo Bugatti exhibits his revolutionary designs at the Exhibition of Decorative Arts in Turin. With the help of Rosenfeld, a European manufacturer, Morimura Gumi produces its first white porcelain.

1903

At Kitty Hawk, North Carolina, the Wright brothers, Orville and Wilber, make the first powered flight in an airplane. On December 17th, the Wright Flyer, powered by a home-made 12 horse power engine, and piloted by Orville, managed to stay in the air for 12 seconds under its own power for a distance of about 40 yards.

Emily Pankhurst starts the "Womens Social & Political Union" which campaigns for universal suffrage for women, while, in Germany, Josef Hofmann & Koloman Moser found the Weiner Werkstatte.

1904

Theodore Roosevelt becomes President of the United States and Charles Rennie Mackintosh designs the Willow Tea Rooms in Glasgow. The Jewel Tea Company is formed in America.

1909

Louis Bleriot makes the first crossing of the English Channel by airplane while, in America, Henry Ford opens the first assembly line for manufacturing cars.

1914

The Panama Canal is opened, saving shipping the 6000 mile trip around Cape Horn to get from the Pacific Ocean to the Atlantic Ocean. This revolutionizes trade between the Orient and Europe. Outbreak of The Great War. Morimura, now Nippon Tokei Kaisha, produce their first porcelain dinner-wares in the European style.

1917

The first recording of jazz music is made by the Dixieland Jazz Band.

1918

Peace is declared, bringing the Great War to an end. British women over thirty are allowed to vote and Walter Gropius founds the German Bauhaus, aiming to bring together form and function in design. This ideal will eventually result in the beginning of the Art Deco movement.

1922

In the Valley of the Kings, near Luxor in Egypt, Howard Carter discovers the tomb of the Pharoah Tutankh-Amen, the boy king who died aged eighteen in 1323 BC. The tomb entrance was discovered on November 4th, and the tomb was opened on the 22nd of that month. The actual burial chamber itself was not breached until February 12th of the following year, but excavations were not finally completed until November 1930. The impact on the world of art and design of this discovery was colossal, and Egyptianesque themes became one of the major motifs of the Art Deco period.

1925

Paris was host to the "Exposition des Arts Decoratifs et Modernes" which became THE showcase for Art Deco style. The new headquarters of the German Bauhaus is designed by Walter Gropius.

1926

Fritz Lang's film "Metropolis" shows an Expressionist vision of the future.

1927

Charles Lindburgh makes the first solo crossing of the Atlantic in his "Spirit of St. Louis." Al Jolson stars in the "Jazz Singer," the first talking film.

1928

In Paris, Pierre Chareau completes his glass and steel "Modernist" house, which typifies "Art Moderne" and is superseding "Art Deco," while, in America, Walt Disney's Mickey Mouse appears for the first time. In Britain, Alexander Fleming discovers penicillin, and the voting age for women is reduced to 21.

1929

This year sees a world-wide depression with massive unemployment.

1932

Franklin D. Roosevelt becomes President of the United States. "Horizon," a treatise on the "streamline" approach to design, is published by Norman Bel Geddes.

1935

The ocean liner S.S. Normandie is finally launched. The ship's interior is the peak in Art Deco design.

1936

King Edward VIII succeeds King George and the British Broadcasting Corporation begin daily radio broadcasts.

1939

The Second World War begins.

We can see that in a comparatively short period of history, the world had seen huge advances in technology which have all had a bearing on the speed of communications. We have gone from a very insular world, where news could take many weeks to travel across the globe to an age of instant communication. Visual arts, such as photography and film, have become commonplace and travel is no longer the huge and time consuming activity that it was. All this meant that advances and innovation in style and fashion became very much a global consideration, and new ideas transmitted quickly across the Atlantic. The late Victorian age saw Britain as the innovator and style leader across the world. The British Empire spanned the globe, and British style was much sought after and much copied. Almost all advances in technology came from Britain and Europe and it was not until after the Great War that Americans also became innovators in style and design in their own right.

The Morimuras, logically, therefore, based their own styles and designs on the European fashion in the early days. We can see how the wares imitated what was fashionable in Europe, starting with wonderful shapes in Moriagewares that were in the Majolica style after the wares coming from Staffordshire factories such as Minton and George Jones.

This moriageware vase captures the Noritake interpretation of majolica style. Komaru mark. 6.75" high. Perfect. £175/200. $250/290.

When the Aesthetic Movement evolved into Art Nouveau, Noritake followed suite, producing wonderfully shaped and decorated pieces in classic shapes, utilizing the rich grounds and styles of the period. We can find pieces hand decorated and gilded on the rich cobalt blues, pinks, and yellow grounds of the British and Continental factories. Much of this output arrived in Europe under the Noritake backstamp, and went to America under a Nippon backstamp.

The lines and decoration of this vase echo Art Nouveau style. Blue mark. 7" high. Perfect. £275/300. $400/450.

The influence of the Arts and Crafts movement was illustrated by a great number of wares that were of simple form and decoration. This movement, dedicated to producing traditionally manufactured goods, simple in shape and decoration, was fairly short-lived in Europe, where the harsh commercial realities of competing against mass produced goods were simply too much for many its exponents. Companies like Liberty, who were able to market affordable silverware with a hand finished appearance simply priced hand made goods out of the popular market. The Arts & Crafts Movement, however, flourished on in America for some time, and the majority of the Noritake wares that were of the style went across the Atlantic.

cal view of the concept. Howard Carter's discoveries in the Valley of the Kings at Luxor fired the imagination and Art Deco style heartily embraced Egyptianesque images and shapes. Noritake, having already produced some wonderful shapes and patterns in the Art Deco vogue, were among the first to follow the new Egyptian format, initially updating their well known "Desert Scene" design with a new gilding format which incorporated Egyptian patterns and a new matte glaze imitative of the Royal Worcester style. The majority of the high Art Deco wares that Noritake produced were for American export, and very few actually came to Europe. The few that did were in the style of two of the foremost Art Deco designers, Susie Cooper and Clarice Cliff.

Typical Arts and Crafts motifs decorate this combination match holder and ashtray. Blue mark. 3" high. Perfect. £85/100. $120/145.

Although the same mold shape as the previous illustration, we can see how the decoration now is in classic early Art Deco style with bold colors and simple decoration reminiscent of Clarice Cliff. Blue mark. 3" high. Perfect. £85/100. $120/145.

Although the first moves in the world of design started firmly in Europe, and many of the German schools were at the forefront of early innovation, the ideals of Art Deco fired the imagination of many American designers, and America at last came into its own as a style leader in this field. Europe had very much its own version of Art Deco design, pursuing more of a Modernist approach, but America embraced the colorful styles and shapes, progressing towards a more radi-

Moving into the late thirties, design became more simplistic, in some cases returning to a form best described as an Art Deco/Art Nouveau hybrid which was simple in style but decorated with floral patterns and gilding. Noritake again moved with the times, producing some innovative pieces reminiscent of the floral style produced by Shelley and Doulton. By 1938 and 1939, the world was taken up with events leading to the second World War, and Noritake's Golden Age was over.

Chapter Five

Collecting Noritake

From a Few Pretty Pieces to a Major Investment

The reason that most people buy a book like this is because they collect, or intend to collect, Noritake porcelain. Collections can take many forms and although some people will just buy anything with the right backstamp, the majority will build a collection along a theme of some kind. It may be a particular pattern, or a certain style, just pairs of vases or coffee cans and saucers or even a specific ground color. There is, however, a common ground, they are all collectors and want the best they can get with the resources at their disposal.

There are some basic rules, which may be useful:

1. Buy the best you can afford

Always try to obtain the best pieces available that fit within your budget. It's not a good idea to spend money you can't spare, and don't risk buying something in the hope of selling it on for a quick profit to another collector. It almost always results in you being stuck with some pieces you didn't really want, and no money to pay the rent! Buy what YOU want, with money you can spare, and leave speculation to the dealers.

2. Start small

If you are a novice Noritake collector, start off with smaller items. Coffee cans and saucers or trinket pots are ideal as they are relatively inexpensive with a wide choice fairly readily available. There is a tremendous range of patterns, colors, and styles. You can build up a nice collection quickly without heavy investment. The other point to note is that if you buy a piece that is not as good as you thought, then you haven't made a huge bad purchase, simply a small one. We all pay to learn and gain experience, so small additions are the best way to go.

3. Learn your subject

It is certainly true that as your collection grows and you gain experience of the wares you begin to pick up this all-important knowledge. You will start to differentiate between the good and the not so good, learn about patterns and shapes, discover what is rare and what isn't and start to find out where to look for new pieces. That, of course, takes time. There is no substitute for experience, but you can gain the basic knowledge very quickly. Knowing the common backstamps may not necessarily enable you to detect restoration on a piece, but you will be able to identify it reasonably accurately, and, more importantly, distinguish good original pieces from copies made by other factories. So read this book from cover to cover, study the pictures, and absorb as much of the basic information as you can. Remember, for every honest and reliable dealer there is one who just wants your money and will tell you what you want to hear to get the sale. If you already know the basics, then it will be a lot easier to ask the right questions when looking to buy a piece. Dealers are simply more honest with people who they perceive to be knowledgeable, and you are far less likely to be sold an inferior piece at an inflated price.

4. Buy the pieces that you like

It is very easy to be pulled into buying for buying's sake. If you have decided on a theme for your collection, then try to stick with it. I'm not suggesting that if you see something unusual that doesn't fit in with that theme then you should pass on it, the rule of "buy what you like" applies to that situation. The trap that collectors so easily fall into is buying a piece because there is nothing else to buy that day. It certainly is disappointing to perhaps travel a long way to an auction or antiques fair only to find that no-one has anything in your pattern, and it becomes very tempting to buy another item which doesn't really fall into your theme simply to justify the time and expense. You can always save the spending money for another day, rather than purchase something that you don't really love and end up with an odd piece on a shelf somewhere. So, buy what you like, but don't just buy because you can.

Avoid buying pieces because they are the "flavor of the month." This is a common pitfall with collecting. Some pieces of a particular style or pattern sell really well at an auction somewhere, or a dealer at an antiques fair sells nine pieces all at once and suddenly that style or pattern becomes "in demand." Prices rise, driven artificially by this demand, and overnight, a middling col lectable pattern is making three or four times the price it was commanding yesterday. A month later, the furor has died down, the pattern falls back to its normal level, and a lot of collectors find themselves with "investment" pieces that will never return what they cost. Noritake, in common with all quality porcelains, rises steadily in value and is always a good long-term investment. Quick price jumps are almost always short term, and very seldom sustainable, so are simply not a good investment as many collectors have found, to their cost.

5. Cultivate your local dealer

Contrary to popular belief, there are a lot of good, honest antiques dealers around and it is well worth finding one or two who know Noritake. If you can find a dealer who is happy to discuss your collection with you—especially the sort of items you are looking for and will buy if the price is right—then, hopefully, your friendly local dealer will do a lot of the work for you. Remember, of course, that the dealer will be going to places that you won't, have a lot of contacts in the antiques world that you won't, and any dealer will be far happier sourcing items that he or she already has a market for. If you have cultivated the person, you will be surprised at how quickly you will start to get calls to pop in and look at a piece or two that "would look nice with your collection." It really means you have another person helping you to collect. If you get to know your dealer, then you can be confident that you will be getting nice pieces at the right price and, should the worst occur, you know where to take the piece back if you have a problem. A good dealer will always be happy to listen to you, and inspect hidden damage that you have found. We're all human, and it is possible to miss restoration or minor damage at first inspection, and sometimes a defect in the piece doesn't become evident until you have, perhaps, given it a good wash, or put it on a shelf where the light strikes it at a different angle, highlighting a small difference in the glaze. If you have a good relationship with your dealer, then it is always possible to return any piece that you are not happy with, as opposed to the problems you may encounter if you have purchased from someone who you don't know. It may be that you bought at an antiques fair, and you will probably have to wait until the next fair at that venue to return the piece. Then, of course, having found your dealer, you then may have to convince that person that: a) they sold you the piece in the first place, and b) you haven't damaged it yourself in the meantime. Remember that receipts are notoriously hard to come by, especially at busy antiques fairs. More on that subject later.

6. Always buy it complete

The hardest job in the known universe is trying to find the sixth cup and saucer to complete a set. If you want to collect sets, then only buy complete sets. It always seems that it will be an easy job to find the odd cup or bowl, but remember this before you buy that set that needs just a milk jug to complete it. Generally speaking, complete sets command a premium on the market, and dealers would far rather sell a complete set, knowing that they will have to reduce the price accordingly if the set they have on the stand is missing odd bits. What happens, therefore, is fairly logical. A dealer will buy an incomplete set, probably quite cheaply, and hang on to it while he or she searches for the missing components.

Remember that dealers will have far more and far better buying opportunities than the average collector, and, of course, a network of colleagues in the trade who will also be on the lookout on their behalf, so they are far more likely than you to complete the set. The partial set, if they have no luck after a period of time, can still be sold on as a partial set or, more probably, split up and sold as individual items to the rest of the dealer network to enable those dealers to complete sets of their own. You may be lucky, but it really will be against the odds to complete a partial set; however, if you have the time, and patience, it can be an interesting, if very long term, project.

7. Keep records

Catalog your collection from the very first piece in as much detail as you can. If possible take photographs of each piece, or use video to record your collection. Buy yourself a good notebook and record every piece, noting where and when you bought it, from whom, the price you paid, and the condition of the piece. Receipts are sometimes hard to come by, but get one if you can. If not, possibly you bought at a fast and furious trade fair or something similar, then get the stand number, as the vendor can always be traced from that if required. Essentially, record everything you can on the piece including dimensions, as they are sometimes hard to infer from a photograph. It is a fact that, should you be unfortunate enough to have items stolen, you stand a far better chance for recovery of your goods if you are able to provide the police with good records. It is also guaranteed that your insurers will thank you for concise details on any claim. It is well worthwhile having your collection insured separately once it grows significantly as some household policies can get tied up in the small print if a collection is stolen. If you are not sure of a correct valuation, contact an expert in the field and have it appraised professionally. If you have been collecting for some time, it may well be that the true value of some of your earlier acquisitions may have increased dramatically which may cause unwanted problems if you find yourself filling in a claim form.

8. Enjoy your collecting

Collecting really should be a hobby, and should be relaxing and enjoyable. Certainly many an antique dealer started by being just a collector and then found that he or she had the opportunity to turn that hobby into a full time job. But, in the main, collecting stays a hobby. So treat it that way. Enjoy your buying trips, finding a piece here and a piece there, negotiating prices, falling upon a real bargain from time to time, and generally enjoying your collection as it grows. The people who collect Noritake come from all walks of life, but have a common interest in the wonderful style and craftsmanship of the wares and that's how it should remain.

So, What Should I Collect?

What to actually collect from the wide and varied range of the Noritake wares is really down to personal choice. It's wise, initially to go for smaller items until you feel confident in the product and have enough experience to go for bigger and better things. Noritake European Export wares can be split into four major areas in terms of pattern and design. These areas are flexible to some extent but everything will generally fit in somewhere.

1. Abstract patterns and gilded patterns

These patterns, generally, are among the easiest styles to find and usually the most inexpensive. Shape does have an effect on this, but more on shapes later. These patterns were generally used on utility and tea wares, so are far more common than the more decorative styles. We would also expect to find the simpler patterns on later pieces, when the output of the factory was responding to the demands of Art Deco style. This style is also more common on the post-war products. A typical example of a perennial favorite from this category is the "Basket of Flowers" pattern No 44318. This pattern, first manufactured in 1906, is still in production today and is probably the most prolific in the U.K.

Some Examples of This Category

Neat and pretty trio in a simple pattern with a nice fluted shape. Blue mark. Perfect. £50/60. $70/85.

Side plate with an abstract pattern and good gilding. 6.6" dia. Perfect. £40/50. $60/70.

Coffee can and saucer in a similar pattern to "Basket of Flowers" known simply as "Raised Gold." Blue mark. Can is 2.25" high. Perfect. £35/45. $50/65.

Pair of vases in a classic Art Nouveau style. Blue mark. 4.25" high. £200/220. $290/325.

2. Floral Patterns

Florals were extremely popular styles throughout the early period, perhaps until the late 1920s. There are a host of patterns from very simple rim patterns to full bodied floral covered pieces. The flowers are virtually all hand painted with roses and chrysanthemums being the most popular. The floral designs are all beautifully executed, and there are stylized patterns as well as the true to life examples. The most popular styles are the larger floral patterns where the flowers are captured in a gilded cartouche on a plain ground of one of the more sought after colors. Cobalt blue is probably the most popular, although the light blue, green, pink, and yellow grounds look stunning. Becoming more popular are the plainer styles, which feature a single type of flower on a plain white ground, very much in the Shelley style of the early thirties. Poppy, tulip, and buttercup are among the nicer examples of this style.

Some Examples of This Category

Typical Noritake floral decorated side plate. Blue mark. 6.5" dia. Perfect. £40/50. $60/70.

Good early floral and gilt trio with interior decoration to the cup. Komaru mark. Perfect. £120/140. $175/210.

Lovely example of a heavily gilded coffee can and saucer in a floral design. Blue mark. Can is 2.25" high. Perfect. £70/80. $100/115.

Classic vase in a floral pattern with good gilding. Blue mark. 7.5" high. Perfect. £240/260. $350/380.

3. Landscapes

Landscapes are, without doubt, the most popular and collectable of the Noritake pattern groups. There are a large number of landscape designs, and many sub-variations, so the choice is almost endless. New landscapes and landscape variations are being discovered regularly, so this category tends to be the most interesting to collect. As such, landscapes are generally of the highest value. These patterns do seem to mainly fall into four types. There are the scenic landscapes, probably led by the "Tree in the Meadow" designs. Tree in the Meadow is generally thought to be one of the patterns created by the company for the Larkin Company, in America, and first made an appearance around 1926. The original design was marketed until around 1935. Other popular landscape patterns include "Swan on the Lake," "Cottage," and several other variations. These designs were used for both utility and fancy wares, so can be found in basic versions and also heavily decorated and gilded versions. They may also be found with luster glazes, following the trend of the mid to late 1930s.

The next category can be loosely grouped as "Japanoiserie." The Japanese culture, steeped in folklore and tradition, forms the basis of this group. Patterns include traditional scenes of old Japanese civilization with geisha girls, willow trees, and Japanese village life. Most of the patterns of this style tend to be grouped under the generic "Geisha Girl" title. There are also a host of patterns based around Japanese mythological creatures. The HoHo or HowHow bird is very popular as is the Japanese dragon, and there are pieces depicting bamboo, the crane bird, and various other plants and animals sacred to Japanese traditions.

Thirdly come the shipping landscapes or, more properly, seascapes. These patterns, which include some of the best and most sought after pieces, are highly decorative and contain some of the best hand painting to be found on Noritake wares. The ships and boats depicted are usually sailing vessels, and there are examples of most types of vessel from simple single masted luggers right through to three masted schooners. There are even examples of Arab dhows.

Finally, there are the exotic landscapes, which are characterized by the immensely popular "Desert Scene," usually known in America as "Man on a Camel." This is the single most collectible pattern found in European export Noritake, and there are at least three different variations, all of which are illustrated later in this book. There are a number of other patterns that fit into this category, in addition to Desert Scene, including landscapes which feature animals. The "Donkey Scene" and "Elephant Scene" are exactly as you would expect, a landscape featuring the animal in question. These are probably the rarest of all the landscapes, and therefore the most valuable and sought after patterns available.

Some Examples of This Category

This coffee can and saucer depict the classic "Swan" scene. Blue mark. Can is 2.25" high. Perfect. £75/85. $110/120.

This cake plate shows a typical traditional landscape design which would fall into the "Geisha Girl" group. Blue mark. 9.75" dia. Perfect. £70/80. $100/120.

A different scenic style is illustrated by this vase. Blue mark. 3" high. Good. £30/35. $45/50.

This section would not be complete without an example of "Desert Scene." This teacup and saucer is in the classic style. Blue mark. Good. £120/140. $175/210.

Miscellaneous and exotic patterns

Perhaps this is a little bit of a cheat, but there are patterns which don't really fall into any of the previous three categories, but are certainly available in Europe. There are a number of pure Art Deco styles and some patterns which are obviously in the American taste and are illustrated and detailed in publications devoted to American export Noritake, complete with American export backstamps. The marketplace began to differ in the early 1920s, and very soon there was an overt difference between the wares destined for America, and the wares destined for Europe. But, some of these patterns appeared, albeit in very small quantities, in Europe complete with a European export backstamp, all of which make these patterns and styles very rare indeed. Without doubt, a certain quantity of American export goods found their way to Europe, hence the information on Nippon elsewhere in this book, but these particular pieces were marked with a European backstamp, which meant that they were destined to be exported directly to Europe. It is even possible to find a very rare piece that bears two backstamps, both an American backstamp and a European backstamp, indicating that the piece was diverted from America to Europe before it left the factory. To the purist, these pieces will be the rarest finds possible.

A very heavily gilded coffee can and saucer on a matte ground typifies high Art Deco style. Blue mark. Can is 2.5" high. Perfect. £75/85. $110/120.

Some Examples of This Category

A very unusual piece is this miniature moriageware child's teacup and saucer from a child's tea set. The pattern is somewhat contentious, but we must remember that the Swastika is an ancient good luck symbol from far before the twentieth century connotation. Blue mark. Cup is 2" high. Good. £70/80. $100/115.

This vase is typical of Art Deco style lusterwares, somewhat reminiscent of contemporary Carltonware style. Green mark. 6.75" high. Perfect £140/160. $210/230.

The reverse of the cake plate,
showing the two backstamps.

This nice quality cake plate is a rarity in European export Noritake. It bears TWO backstamps, a Noritake Nippon mark, which is American and ALSO a green Komaru mark which is European. The piece was originally destined for the American market, but diverted, probably to fill a European export order, and marked accordingly. The plate is otherwise a completely standard, well decorated and gilded 9.75" cake plate in perfect condition. £225/250. $325/375.

So, having categorized the types and styles in terms of patterns, it would be worthwhile to consider the shapes available in these patterns. To do that, we must firstly realize that there are two different types of wares, which are the Utility wares and the Fancies. Utility wares are items designed for normal day to day use in a household such as tea sets, coffee sets, dinner services, and general kitchenwares. We must, however, include a number of other items that would have been regarded as utility wares eighty or a hundred years ago when lifestyles were quite different. Quite common in a middle class household in that period would be cuspidors or spittoons, egg warmers, knife rests, individual salts, mustache cups, and hatpin holders. Ashtrays would be an integral part of the drawing room equipment with big indentations for cigars rather than cigarettes. Smoking accessories were very common, from match holders to large, ornate humidors and cigarette boxes. Writing was a far more common pastime than it is today, and desk sets were in every day use, complete with inkwells. On the dining table there would often be a condensed milk container, often highly decorative with its own lid, and easily identified today by the hole in the bottom, left to enable the user to push the tin back out when it was empty, and the hostess would usually provide small semi-circular dishes for each guest. These small dishes fitted neatly around the rear edge of the dinner plate to collect bones and inedible scraps during the meal. The quality of decoration of these items, and indeed the complete sets, varied according to the individual's taste and pocket, but now offer a wealth of opportunity to the collector.

"Fancies" is a general term for decorative items. This would include vases, figurines, lamps, and novelty items. I would also put cabinet wares into this category. Cabinet wares are simply highly decorated utility wares, plates, and cups, etc. that are designed for display rather than use. One could also put in this category items or sets which, although strictly should be classed as utility items, by virtue of their actual utilization were generally highly decorative. Calling card trays were popular, and usually very highly decorated as a small indication of status, and also vanity sets or dressing table sets would be destined for a feminine boudoir, and would be very pretty.

Very often, a collector will have parts of a set of some kind in the collection without realizing that originally these items were part of a set. Small trinket dishes, ring trees, inkwells, hatpin holders, and cigarette boxes all started life in a set, which has become split over the years and now provides the collector with a ready supply of small, inexpensive decorative items.

So, there is a virtually infinite variety of patterns and shapes to choose from and the values vary accordingly. The new collector can start, literally, with a few pounds and pick up neat coffee cans and saucers in simple gilded designs, and work steadily up to something like a complete coffee set or dressing table set in Desert Scene pattern for well over a thousand pounds. Just work within your budget, perhaps try a theme for your collection, but do collect the pieces that you like!

Where Is the Best Place to Buy Noritake?

There are a number of obvious sources of Noritake, and one or two that may not be quite as obvious. Which of these sources you try will depend on what you are looking for in terms of price, and on how much experience of the wares you have.

1. Auction houses

Auction houses can have Noritake of all styles and qualities, and it is sometimes a good source of cheaper pieces. Buying at auction is fairly straightforward, and most good auction houses will be happy to explain the procedure if you are a new buyer. If you are planning to try this source, then there are a few points to remember. You don't pay the price you bid as auction houses add their commission to the hammer price, and depending on where you are, this could be anything up to an extra 20%, although the average is around 10%, plus any sales taxes that apply. This means that you have to account for commissions when deciding how much to bid. Discipline is very important in an auction. It is very easy to get carried away in the heat of the moment, and get into a duel with another buyer, resulting in you paying far too much for the item, just to beat the other person. If you are going to bid, set your limit, allowing for the commissions, and stick to it. If the item goes past your limit, let it go and try on something else. If you are to bid at an auction, attend in person. Proxy or commission bidding is common, and some auction houses will allow you to bid on the telephone, but if you haven't inspected and examined the pieces, then you really are taking a huge risk. Most auction houses will give you a condition report over the telephone, and more and more houses have on-line facilities so can email you a picture of items that you are interested in, but this can be a problem. No auction house will deliberately mislead a potential customer, but condition reports are subjective. The house wants to sell the piece for the highest price possible, so wants as many people as possible bidding; therefore, any description over the telephone will be aimed at making the piece sound as attractive as possible. What does "minimal wear" on the gilding really mean? You may think that minimal wear means that the wear is hardly noticeable, but the auction house may think that this means that at least some of the gilding is still there, so you could get this piece only to find that you consider the wear on the gilding to be very bad. You, of course, are now stuck with piece because the auction house will not take it back.

The other problem is damage or restoration. The auction house will be very busy, and probably banging out verbal condition reports every few minutes on various items, so your piece will probably, at best, only get a cursory inspection and the person talking to you may honestly not spot any small damage or restoration, especially if the restoration has been done well. This could well mean that you are paying a premium price for what you perceive as a perfect piece only to find later that it is not perfect. Once again, there will be no redress as the condition report was verbal, and the house will take no responsibility.

One must even beware of viewing the lots a couple of days before the auction date, and leaving commission bids. The problem here is that a lot of other people will have handled the goods after you have examined them, and the items may have sustained damage in the interim, so, once again, you are bidding, via the auctioneer, on an item that was perfect when you examined it, but is now in three pieces. Just a small point to finish this: most auction houses are good, honest businesses with auctioneers who are very professional; but, there are some that may not reach that high standard, so you may get misleading information and artificial bidding where item prices are pushed up by fictitious commission bids. The last point to bear in mind is that some dealers will put pieces that have been restored into auction to clear them without any comebacks from buyers. If you think that the estimate or reserve on a piece seems very low, especially if you recognize it to be quite rare, check it and check again, there will probably be something wrong with it. Most auction houses will assign a realistic value to the piece, but THEY ARE NOT OBLIGED TO TELL YOU IF THERE IS ANYTHING WRONG WITH IT. In the auction system, "Caveat Emptor" applies with a vengeance. This means, literally "let the buyer beware," so you must satisfy yourself as to the condition of the piece you want to buy, and if you get it wrong, the house may be sympathetic but they won't refund your money unless their description of the piece was fundamentally wrong.

So, auction houses can be a good source, but be very careful. Unless you are an experienced collector, avoid the big money pieces.

2. Antique Fairs

Antique fairs are certainly the best places to buy Noritake. There can be a lot of choice and a wide range of prices, especially at the larger "trade" fairs. You really have to know a little about the wares, however, if you want to find real bargains. There are definitely two categories of fair, and both have their own advantages and disadvantages. It is very much a question of approaching each type of fair slightly differently, dependent upon what you are actually looking to buy. The majority of antique fairs tend to be small affairs, maybe up to 100 or so exhibitors, most of which are part time antique dealers who use the trade as a hobby for a little extra income. Generally, the quality of goods is rather poor, mostly cheap or modern wares, so really these tend to be collectors fairs rather than antiques fairs proper. Having said that, there certainly can be bargains at these fairs as, in general, the dealers or exhibitors carry a potpourri of stock of all kinds and quite often don't really know much about the stock they are displaying other than the manufacturer and maybe some very basic information on the piece. Quite often there, amongst the diverse display, a keen eye may spot the odd piece of Noritake, which will probably have a bargain price tag. Most small dealers at these fairs work simply on a profit rather than appraising the piece and pricing it at the correct level, so you will, generally, pay less here. Obviously, the bargains can be hard to find as the majority of the Noritake wares at these small fairs are at the cheaper end of the price spectrum; however, it is an ideal training ground for the novice collector as it is unlikely that top quality wares will be found, so there will be no big price tags. Do check very carefully for damage, however, as quite often there will be a lot of inferior stock but it is a worthwhile exercise in itself if you can start to recognize the distinctive Noritake style from within a stall full of wares, and, more importantly, start to be familiar with the common forms of damage found on old porcelain. Also remember that many of the bigger dealers use these smaller fairs as shopping territory as well, and as they are in the trade, have probably got into the fair before the public is admitted to have look around, so don't expect, unless you are very lucky, to pick up a rare piece for nothing.

The bigger regional and national antiques fairs are a different story. In addition to the general ceramics dealers, there will be specialist dealers and, certainly in the U.K., most big fairs will have two or three specialist Noritake dealers. The dealers who exhibit at the bigger fairs will usually be much more knowledgeable, and it is fair to say that you will pay the market rate for pieces. Exhibiting at these fairs is expensive, and beyond the financial reach of all but the bigger dealers so bargains will be rare; however, if you want to be sure of quality and to be able to discuss what you are buying in detail, then this is the place to go. The vast majority of the bigger fairs now have a serious quality policy, and most have a vetting system which entails a panel of experts checking the stock to be exhibited to ensure that it is of sufficiently high quality, labeled and dated correctly, and that the dealers know what they are doing.

So, you have a choice with antique fairs, either the smaller events where you can pick up bargains—but you must know your stuff if you are to be successful—or the larger fairs where you will pay the going rate, but will have confidence that what you are buying is good quality. The last bit of advice here is to try both and see what suits you. If you are a new collector, it is nice to try out your new knowledge at the smaller fairs where you won't have to have a bottomless money pit; but, if you are looking at better pieces and the budget is higher, go to a larger fair and talk to a specialist.

3. The Internet

This huge growth area cannot be ignored. You, literally, have a worldwide marketplace at your fingertips and the number of on-line auctions and Internet marketplaces grows daily. The range and quantity of Noritake on offer is huge, with some of the larger Internet auctions listing almost 1000 items at any one time. We discussed buying part sets and suggested that the chances of completing one is remote, but the Internet will probably offer the best chance of finding the odd piece to finish that set, should you take the risk. Provided you have a computer and access to the Internet it all seems very easy, but is it?

The problems associated with buying on-line are similar to those with buying from an unviewed auction. You basically have to rely on pictures and the vendor's description to decide whether or not to buy and you don't actually get your hands on the piece until you have paid for it. I emphasize that the vast majority of vendors are honest people who wouldn't dream of cheating a buyer but all the problems of subjective descriptions apply, and remember that a good imaging program on a decent computer can make just about anything look good. There are also major problems associated with buying internationally; the biggest one is, of course, that an unscrupulous vendor will know that you won't perhaps travel from England to America or vice versa to dispute a £50 purchase. There are also problems of monetary exchange; remember that other countries don't have a clearing bank system as in the U.K. and personal checks can take months to clear, so you could be waiting for your purchase to arrive for a long time. Shipping the goods internationally can also cause problems, as can International insurance facilities, as some countries have very complex systems or they are simply non-existent. This can lead to all sorts of difficulties as parcels do vanish in the postal system, or can arrive badly damaged or even empty, the goods having been removed in transit. We should also be aware that the Customs organizations of most countries take a very keen interest in the transit of antiques and collectibles, and all too often that reasonably priced piece costs a lot more than you thought once the shipping charges, import duties, and sales taxes have been added.

For all of that, there is still a place for Internet trading, but be aware of the problems, and take all the precautions that you can before committing yourself to a purchase. There are some simple safeguards that can minimize the risks if you use them, and it's worth that little extra effort. If you are considering bidding on or buying a piece on-line, see what checks you can make on the vendor. Quite often there is a feedback system in use as part of the auction facilities where other buyers have left comments about the vendor. Have a read through any previous comments to check the vendor's previous record, and if there is any history of previous problems, then don't bid or buy.

Use your email facility to ask any relevant questions that aren't covered by the item description. Don't be afraid to ask direct questions about damage or restoration if it's not mentioned, as sometimes a vendor may "forget" to mention a chip until it's too late, and will then simply say that you didn't ask at the time.

Ask the vendor to give you an estimate on the shipping costs through a reputable international carrier such as UPS or DHL. It will cost more than normal postage, but the goods will be properly looked after in transit and you will have some form of redress if there are any problems.

Finally, if available, especially on larger or more expensive items, use an "escrow" system. This is a simple system whereby the escrow agent will take your payment, inform the vendor that they have the payment in trust, and the vendor will then ship you the goods. Once you have examined the goods and are satisfied, the escrow agent releases the payment to the vendor. Some escrow agents will even arbitrate in cases of dispute. There is usually a small fee involved, and shipping is slower, but it is the safest way to make your purchase. If this facility is not available, then pay with a credit card if you possibly can. It certainly speeds up the overall transaction, and if there is a dispute, then the credit card company will intervene on your behalf, should you be unable to settle things yourself. Do ensure, however, that you take precautions when sending credit card information over the Internet. It is possible for your card number and details to be intercepted and then used illegally without your knowledge; so, if at all possible use a Secure Server system (SSL) to transmit the information, or, at the very least, send the information split up over several different emails over a two or three hour period. This will lessen the chances of interception considerably.

So, provided you are aware of the situation and use as many of these safeguards as you can, the Internet is a very good place to look for Noritake. One final point worth mentioning, however. If you are collecting European export Noritake specifically, remember that the majority of the items on offer will probably be from one of the overseas export markets, so keep your backstamp book to hand, and do ask for a picture of the backstamp if it's not available with the item description.

4. Antique shops and independent dealers

Very similar to the antiques fairs in many ways, shops can be a very good source for Noritake, especially the larger antique centers that may have a number of independent dealers all under one roof. The good thing is that you can build up a relationship with the owner(s) and get them looking for pieces for you. Of course the limitation is that a town may only have one or two shops or centers, so calling on several will entail a lot of traveling around the region and stocks in antique shops and centers don't turn over as quickly as at antique fairs where the dealers exhibiting quite often change from fair to fair. You may be lucky enough to find a Noritake specialist in a local shop or center, but usually these operations have to be generalist to attract a wide range of customers. Unless you can cultivate a particular dealer, as we have mentioned previously, then it's simply a question of calling regularly and letting everyone know that you collect and are always interested, should anything come into the shop or center.

Antique shops and centers are nice because you can build up relationships, but, unless you have a sympathetic dealer, it's often a waiting game.

5. Collector's Clubs

Most collectible items or wares will have a collector's club, and Noritake is no exception. Most countries will have their own club, and if you are going to be serious about collecting Noritake you should join. There is usually a small annual fee, which will get you a regular newsletter and other benefits such as reduced or free entry to some antiques fairs but more importantly, you will be associated with other people with the same interest as you. There is normally a classified section in the newsletter for members to buy, sell, and swap items and a wanted section where you can advertise for any specific items you are looking for. All of these offerings are private among the club members, so you would stand a far better chance of obtaining particular pieces, patterns, or styles in a club than in the public arena. Quite often Noritake specialist dealers are among the membership, and there are usually special discounts for other club members, and those dealers speak the same language as you. You will find that they will be happy to look out for pieces for you, more so than general antique dealers because if they source an item which is not exactly what you want, there are still all the other members to sell it on to.

The other big advantage of belonging to a collector's club is that you have a ready source of information on the wares. Most clubs offer an information and research service to members so you have a ready ear to listen to your queries, and someone who can identify pieces for you, advise you on current market values, and even inspect potential purchases for you. There is also expert advice in cases of dispute, which may solve potential problems regarding insurance values or even identifying fake or copy pieces. The small fee that a collector's club charges will repay itself time and time again if you take the time to join.

How Do I Know if I'm Paying a Fair Price?

This is the one area that a book really can't answer. If you feel comfortable with the price and you are happy to part with that amount of money for that piece, then the price is probably right, is the glib and simple answer. If only it were that simple, or we all had a price list for Noritake, then the problem wouldn't arise, but of course, it simply isn't that simple. In reality the price will depend on a number of factors, and pure experience is, of course, the overriding one. When a long term collector looks at a piece with experienced eyes, then the value of the piece becomes self evident, and a quick check of the price tag will reveal that the figure there is too high, about right, or is a bargain! What we should consider are the factors that come into play in making that decision.

1. Condition

This is the major factor in valuing an item, and upon which everything else hangs. The first thing to look for is damage or restoration. Is there any damage? Is it major or minor, and how does it affect you? Some collectors can accommodate minor damage provided it doesn't affect the appearance, and others will not accept anything less than perfect, so that's a subjective thing. Restoration is the other element that affects collectors in different ways. Minor restoration, well executed, should not be visible except possibly under the most critical examination, and should not change the appearance of the piece. Such minor restoration is usually acceptable but, again, it's subjective. Minor, in the context of damage or restoration, would be to a very small area of the piece: for example, a chip under the base or foot rim or a very faint hairline that is barely visible. Any damage or restoration that is obvious in a cursory inspection of the piece should not be accepted as minor, but it's a subjective thing, once again.

Wear is another area for consideration. We must remember that the majority of the popular Noritake wares are in excess of seventy years old, and we must take this age into account. The gilding on any piece is the most prone area to wear as the material is comparatively soft and has probably been dusted many thousands of times, each time taking a minuscule amount of gold away until, eventually, it becomes thin enough to see the underlying porcelain ground. Unless one is very lucky, virtually every piece will have some wear somewhere, and we must consider what is acceptable. Minor wear should really be only discernible on the protrud-

ing areas of the piece, the knop on a lid, or the top of the cup handle being the most prone. A thinning of the gilt on these and similar areas, with the odd small area of the body showing through is acceptable, but huge areas of gilt completely missing certainly do not come into this definition. Regilding is a related area worthy of comment. In general, regilding is fairly obvious, is virtually never as good as the original, and so sticks out like the proverbial sore thumb. Done well, regilding is marginally acceptable, again if we are considering a very small area, but otherwise should not be considered as minor. Quite often regilding hides a greater sin, so always be very wary that this work does not attempt to conceal a major repair.

Overall condition is very difficult to define into a number of categories or levels as, in reality, it all depends on subjective assessment of the piece in question. That which one collector may regard as minor wear, another would consider to be considerably worn, and, of course, our perception of damage or wear will change with experience or even if we take into consideration the relative value of the piece. A degree of wear that a collector might find unacceptable in, say, a simple trinket pot in a basic floral pattern could well be tolerable if that piece was in the very rare Elephant pattern. As a rough but workable guide, we can attempt a categorization as follows:

1. Perfect

No damage or restoration. No wear on the gilding or paintwork. All in original condition and possibly with original box if applicable.

2. Good

No damage or restoration. Minor wear, as we have discussed, to protrusions, handles, or rims. Most Noritake pieces will fall into this category.

3. Average

Minor damage, to the level we have already discussed. Minor restoration, executed well. Minor wear.

4. Poor

Major damage, this defines as larger chips or cracks, but with all the pieces in place. Major or obvious restoration or repairs. Heavy wear on large areas of the gilding.

From all this, we can arrive at a decision regarding the condition, and what will be acceptable to us. Generally, Perfect or Good will be suitable for most pieces and most collectors. If, however, we are looking at a piece in Average condition, then rarity and desirability will come into play, having much more of an influence. Pieces in poor condition will not usually be acceptable, but rarity and desirability would affect any decision to buy.

As we have mentioned, rarity will certainly affect the price, although desirability is a personal thing. A collector may happily pay a higher price for an item that will compliment a particular part of the collection, or add to a set, but may not be prepared to pay the asking price for a stand alone item. Rarity, if we disregard "flavor of the month" trends, breaks down to shape and pattern.

The patterns, in the main, run fairly smoothly, in terms of rarity, from the simple abstract and gilded works, through the florals to the landscapes. The anomaly, of course, is the miscellaneous and exotic category, which can fall into any area of the rarity spectrum. Unusual American Export patterns and shapes such as inkwells or powder bowls in the shape of crinoline ladies, for example, would be quite rare and be in the same range as Desert Scene or Shipping patterns. Any of the American export patterns bearing European backstamps such as those depicting Art Deco lady figures are extremely rare, on the level of Elephant or Donkey pattern, but heavy Art Nouveau patterns in the style of William Morris, although very colorful, and quite rare, are not terribly popular, so would fall into the same area as the floral patterns.

Shape is the other consideration when contemplating the value of a piece. The utility wares would logically be expected to be cheaper than fancies, and this is certainly true of the less desirable patterns and standard tea and dinnerware shapes; but, remember we discussed the more unusual items which fall into this category, such as smoking sets and desk sets, which, if complete, will command a higher price, as will complete tea or coffee sets with the rarer patterns. Cabinet pieces are always very desirable, especially if they are in perfect or good condition, and pairs of vases are always in demand. A word here on pairs of vases, mirror imaged decoration is far more desirable, and would be worth more than two vases with the same pattern, so be sure to check the pattern carefully.

Other items that, in original form, are quite rare are lamp bases. Noritake did produce complete original lamp bases for European export, so do check if you are considering purchasing one of these highly sought after pieces as later conversions, whilst quite acceptable if done properly, should not command as high a price as the original factory manufactured examples. One can find, on the rare occasion, a garniture set, which was designed to sit on a Victorian or Edwardian sideboard or mantelpiece. This would be a pair of vases, sometimes mirrored, and a centerpiece of some kind, which could take the form of a lamp base, a fruit bowl, or a vase of a different shape (such as a three-handled version) carrying the same pattern as the pair. Many garnitures have been split up over the years, so a complete set will be a rarity.

So, to arrive at a value, hence a selling price for a piece or set, we have to take into consideration the condition, pattern, shape, rarity, and, of course, the desirability. But, is it a fair price? We really are back to experience to determine that, but you can get an idea of whether that is realistic in several ways. Is the dealer a specialist in Noritake? Are there similar pieces on other stands, or in other shops, with similar prices? All dealers will usually negotiate on price a little, but did the vendor drop a long way very quickly? Have you bought a similar piece recently? Are you able to call the collector's club to get an idea of the current value of that kind of item? If you are talking to a specialist dealer, then the price is probably going to be about right for that piece at that time. If there are other pieces which are comparable in style and quality you can look at, and the prices are reasonably close, then you are looking good. If the dealer has made a big drop in asking price, then beware. Check the piece out carefully and ask again about damage or restoration, but don't write it off, it may be that the dealer has realized that it's a bit over priced and is rectifying it with his reduction, or it may be that it has been around for a while, and it's been priced down to make the sale. If you are buying similar pieces for a themed collection, and the asking price is around the same level, then you will know that it is right. Finally, if you are considering buying a rare or expensive piece or set and you are a member of the collector's club, it's always worth a quick telephone call for independent advice on current pricing levels. I doubt they would thank you for asking advice on a piece worth a few pounds, but if you are considering investing a lot of money, then they will certainly be able to tell you at what level the item you are considering should be priced.

In the final analysis, however, the decision to buy is yours, and half the fun and enjoyment in collecting is the thrill of adding a new item to your collection. Provided you keep within your budget, remember a few of the basic guidelines, and feel yourself that the piece is worth the asking price, then you won't go far wrong.

Building and Caring for Your Collection

Silly as it sounds, especially to a new collector, knowing what to actually do with your collection as it grows can be a real problem. At first, a few nice little pieces live on shelves or on mantelpieces, but it can get out of hand very quickly. It's wise to consider how you are going to accommodate your collection as it grows, and in which direction you will go. Many people start with a neat collection of coffee cans and saucers, then graduate into buying complete sets, only to discover that it's much harder to display a coffee set, which needs much more room. Collections are meant to be looked at and enjoyed, so display is very important. Well-lit china cabinets are ideal, but ensure, if you can, that the cabinet or cabinets are not in direct sunlight. Cabinets protect your Noritake from dust and atmospheric changes, but direct sunlight through the glass case can create extreme conditions of heat and light that will affect the glaze and gilding. Open display locations are fine, and it's often easier to display larger items on shelves or tabletops.

It is best not to wash finely decorated porcelain too often, but a rinse in warm water with a non-detergent soap liquid will do it no harm. Feather dusters are ideal (rather than cloth) for keeping the pieces fresh, but it's mainly down to common sense concerning frequency of cleaning, as the less the pieces are handled the better. If you are having a change around in your display, remember to wash your hands as the acids present on your skin will, in the long term, affect the gilding.

Quite often, as your collection grows, especially if you have limited display space, you will find yourself storing some items as you add to your collection or change your display. Always wrap your pieces, individually, in acid free tissue before you put them away. Normal tissue paper contains acids that will, over a period of time, affect the glaze and gilding, and, in extreme cases, leach the actual color from the piece. Bad storage is, in fact, one of the major causes of wear on the older Noritake wares.

Finally, remember that collecting Noritake is one of the few enjoyable and relaxing pastimes that can actually make you money. Noritake porcelain has increased in value many times over in the last twenty years, and values, especially of the rarer pieces, continue to grow quickly as the popularity and recognition of the quality of the wares increases. There is no doubt that in their heyday the Noritake factories were producing quality porcelain equal to anything from the English and continental manufacturers, but only in recent years has the demand risen to a level that has put Noritake in it's rightful place as their equal.

Chapter Six

Introduction to the Picture Section

The following chapters contain, exclusively, pictures of European export Noritake, all exhibiting one of the four recorded European export backstamps in use between the mid-1890s and 1939.

There are a number of points which must be borne in mind when using the picture section and a certain amount of explanation is required to understand the captioning. Each caption contains information on the piece: size(s), the backstamp, condition, and a price guide both in Pounds Sterling and United States dollars.

Description

The content of each picture is self evident, so descriptions are brief, but include any point of interest that will differentiate a particular item from others similar in form. The rarer and more desirable patterns are noted and also any rare or unusual features. There are also notes regarding origins, especially if an individual item was originally part of a larger set.

Sizes

Where appropriate, sizes are part of the picture caption and are approximate. Many of the shapes are very difficult to measure accurately, and the sizes quoted are to give an indication of relative size only. If there are a number of items of the same type, then the size will generally only be included in the first example. If the picture is of multiple items, a tea set, for example, then there will be an indication of the size of the most significant item, and the rest of the relative sizes may be inferred from that.

Backstamp

The backstamp for every piece is indicated. The backstamp is one of four, and is abbreviated as follows:

Blue Komaru mark will be "Blue mark"
Green Komaru mark will be "Green mark"
Red Komaru mark will be "Red mark"

The plain blue Komaru mark with no text will be "Komaru mark"

Any exceptions to this are noted in the individual item descriptions.

Condition

Condition of the pieces illustrated is indicated, using a basic quality system.

"Perfect" is without wear or damage, and with original packaging where indicated.

"Good" is without damage but some minimal wear to the high spots on the gilding, i.e. knops or handles.

"Average" is with some wear to the gilding or decoration and/or some minimal damage or restoration.

On some items there may be a component part missing, the insert in a butter tub, for example. Although this is not strictly a condition issue, it is indicated in the description and the value adjusted accordingly.

Price Guide

There is a value shown for each item or set. This value applies to that piece or set in the condition indicated, and will vary by anything up to 25% higher or lower according to the relative condition of any actual item. Condition is a subjective opinion and these values, therefore, are A GUIDE, NOT A PRICE LIST.

The first value quoted, in Pounds Sterling, is based on United Kingdom retail values. The second value, in United States Dollars, is not an American retail valuation as the American Noritake market is based very much on American export Noritake and Noritake Nippon which is fundamentally different to Europe. Pieces, which have quite low valuations for the European market may command far higher prices in America and vice versa. The Dollar valuation in this book is, therefore, a simple conversion to American currency.

In some instances, a picture may not show a complete set, in which case the valuation is based for the complete set, as indicated in the caption.

Chapter Seven

Plates

As displaying plates properly requires a lot of space, they are not the most popular collector's items, although they are probably the most prolific items available. A standard Noritake full dinner service would be for twelve and would contain something in the order of seventy-five plates and platters, and specialist additional items could well take the total to over eighty. The standard plate sizes produced by Noritake are:

Dinner Plate	9.75 inches diameter
Breakfast Plate	8.5 inches diameter
Tea Plate	7.5 inches diameter
Soup Underplate	7.0 inches diameter
Side Plate	6.5 inches diameter
Fruit Plate	5.25 inches diameter

A dinner service would also normally include a graduated set of meat platters, three in total and oval in shape: 16" x 12", 14" x 10", and 12" x 9".

In addition to the standard plate sets, there are also a number of "specialist" plates and platters, designed for specific purposes. The cake plate was circular with small side handles and could be nine, ten, or eleven inches in diameter, the larger size often doubling as a cold meat platter. Sandwich plates were available, normally in the ten-inch size, sometimes with a raised pillar handle in the center for passing around. Noritake also produced a square form fruit or cake plate, usually 8 inches, again with a pair of small handles, and a number of oblong platters with small raised handles for asparagus or corn-on-the-cob.

Not all plates were simple round forms: square, octagonal, and oblong varieties were produced along with items with squat raised bases, around an inch in height as part of dessert sets, and many had forms of relief or blown out decoration.

The majority of plates available were simple utility wares, but Noritake did produce a number of wall plates purely as decorative pieces. These wall plates were normally quite small, 8.5 or 7.5 inch diameter was usual, but the base was drilled to take a wire hanger.

As with other utility wares, plates were also produced as cabinet pieces, highly decorative and designed for display rather than use, and these cabinet plates are now very much sought after as collector's pieces. Always be aware that most plates, other than cabinet plates, will probably show signs of wear, especially in the center where, quite often, knife marks will show quite clearly if the plate is tilted to the light. Plates, in general, with the exception of the cabinet examples, do not command the highest prices, therefore restoration is fairly uncommon, but as utility items, they should be examined carefully for damage.

Side plate. Blue mark. 6.5" dia. Good. £20/30. $30/45.

Side plate. Blue mark. 6.5" dia. Good. £30/40. $45/60.

Side plate. Blue mark. 6.5" dia. Perfect. £30/40. $45/60.

Side plate. Blue mark. 6.5" dia. Perfect. £45/55. $65/80.

Twelve sided side plate. Blue mark. 6.5" dia. Perfect. £35/45. $50/65.

Side plate. Blue mark. 6.5" dia. Perfect. £45/55. $65/80.

Side plate. Blue mark. 6.5" dia. Perfect. £45/55. $65/80.

Good scenic side plate. Blue mark. 6.5" dia. Perfect. £60/70. $85/100.

Scenic side plate. Blue mark. 6.5" dia. Good. £15/25. $20/35.

Side plate. Blue mark. 6.5" dia. Perfect. £50/60. $70/85.

Scenic side plate. Blue mark. 6.5" dia. Good. £15/25. $20/35.

Pair of scenic fruit plates. Blue mark. 5.25" dia. Perfect. The pair £120/140. $175/210.

Good side plate in Desert Scene. Blue mark. 6.5" dia. Perfect. £80/100. $115/145.

Side plate. Blue mark. 6.5" dia. Perfect. £30/40. $45/60.

Side plate in Desert Scene with matte finish. Blue mark. 6.5" dia. Perfect. £125/135. $180/200.

Tea plate. Blue mark. 7.5" dia. Perfect. £60/70. $85/100.

Tea plate in Desert Scene. Blue mark. 7.5" dia. Perfect. £120/140. $175/210.

Tea plate. Blue mark. 7.5" dia. Good. £60/70. $85/100.

Good scenic tea plate. Blue mark. 7.5" dia. Perfect. £175/200. $250/290.

Very good heavily gilded cabinet plate. Blue mark. 7.5" dia. Perfect. £180/200. $260/290.

Lobed floral dinner plate. Blue mark. 10" dia. Good. £80/100. $115/145.

Dinner plate. Blue mark. 10" dia. Good. £80/100. $115/145.

Lobed floral dinner plate. Komaru mark. 10" dia. Good. £90/110. $125/160.

Good scenic cabinet plate.
Blue mark. 10" dia. Perfect.
£180/200. $260/290.

Cake plate. Blue mark. 10" dia. Perfect. £100/125. $145/180.

Good scenic cabinet plate. Blue mark. 10" dia. Perfect. £175/225.
£250/325.

48

Cake plate. Green mark. 9.75" dia. Perfect. £220/240. $320/350.

Cake plate. Blue mark. 10" dia. Perfect. £150/180. $220/260.

Good scenic cake plate. Blue mark. 9.75" dia. £200/220. $290/320.

Square cake plate in Desert Scene. Blue mark. 9.5" dia. Perfect. £250/275. $325/395.

Chapter Eight

Tea, Coffee, Chocolate Sets, and Related Items

This is by far the biggest picture section in the book, not surprisingly as hot beverage sets were a major sales story in Europe for Noritake. Each set was comprised of a minimum of fifteen pieces, excluding lids, and a full tea set would normally have forty-three components, again, excluding lids. Of course, the archetypal gift for any occasion would be a tea or coffee set, and Noritake even supplied boxed presentation and gift sets.

Tea sets or tea services were extremely popular throughout the late nineteenth and early twentieth century. Curiously, teapots were not considered essential components of a tea set for every day domestic use until well into the twentieth century. There would be a large family teapot which would hold far more than the small teapots available with the set, and this would be used on a daily basis, with the teapot, if indeed there was one, would only be used for entertaining guests, when tea became more of a social grace than a thirst quenching beverage. Most early Noritake teapots are, for that reason, comparatively small, and capable of holding only three or four cups at the most.

In Victorian and Edwardian times families were generally larger, and a full tea set at that time would be quite a comprehensive array of porcelain. There would usually be twelve cups, saucers, and side plates, a milk jug, a sugar bowl, two cake or bread and butter plates, a slop bowl, a hot water jug, and, if required, a teapot. The slop bowl is often mistaken for a large sugar basin, but sugar was an expensive commodity, and the sugar basin was always quite a small bowl, and quite often had a lid. The slop bowl was usually around six inches in diameter, and was used to pour the tea dregs into before refilling the teacup. Tea was not as well refined, and the tannin in the dregs would make a refill taste bitter so custom was to empty out the slops before a fresh cup was poured. Sugar bowls themselves had undergone a quiet revolution in shape and form; the earliest sugar bowls from the eighteenth century were large affairs, maybe up to eight inches in diameter and always lidded. Sugar was then imported in "loaf" form as a large solid chunk, and it was broken down with a small hammer into manageable sizes so the sugar bowl had to be big enough to take the resultant sugar "lumps." By the end of the nineteenth century, sugar was refined into the granulated form we know today, but was then invariably cast back into small cubes. Sugar was still very expensive so the bowls got smaller to take just a small number of sugar cubes. The domestic atmosphere was generally damp from open fires and lids were still employed to keep the sugar from absorbing water vapor from the air and becoming damp itself.

It is almost possible, therefore, to date a tea set just by looking at the component parts rather than the backstamp. In early utility tea sets from Noritake, the form was very plain, just a simple dished cup with a loop handle. The saucers and plates were regular with no fluting and the decoration was usually a simple rim decoration with some gilding and maybe a small transfer print motif. The milk jug would be quite large, maybe up to 5 inches in height, and the sugar bowl may or may not have a cover. The hot water jug would always have a cover, and there will be a slop bowl, up to seven inches in diameter, but probably not a teapot or bread and butter plate.

Example of a typical early trio with transfer print decoration. Blue mark. Good condition. £30/40. $45/60.

Later into the period, as we come to the 1930s, the forms will change. Afternoon tea has become a social ritual and tea sets have become far more decorative in form and pattern, with fluting, much heavier gilding and full patterns, including some work on the inside of the cups. The sets, however, are all far more delicate, quite often in pedestal form, with the cups, jugs, and teapots all standing on a single pedestal leg. These sets were meant to be seen as well as used with hostesses engaged in the time-honored ritual of outdoing each other in the entertaining stakes. Afternoon tea was seen the world over as an essentially English ceremony, so the vast majority of teawares were of traditional form and pattern with very few of the more avant-garde shapes appearing in Europe.

Coffee sets can be simply distinguished from tea sets. A coffee set is always for six, and comprises six cups or cans and saucers, a coffee pot, cream jug, and sugar bowl. The coffee pot is a tall vessel with a long spout and the cream jug and sugar bowl are quite small. Coffee cups are smaller than teacups, and the commonest shape is the cylindrical coffee can. Coffee sets were not widely in use in most households until the late nineteenth century, although coffee had been commonly available since the seventeenth century.

The custom of the coffee house was an old tradition that took the social revolutions of the late nineteenth and early twentieth century to become popular domestically. Coffee was far more of a social beverage than one in everyday use for most people, so coffee sets were not as big and successful commercially as tea sets. As coffee was more popular with the younger generations, the styles and patterns tended to be more decorative although many examples of plainer utility sets exist.

Coffee sets became a popular gift, and boxed sets were supplied to meet the giftware demand. Most boxed sets would include six coffee cans and saucers, and quite often six spoons. These spoons would usually be silver, or sometimes enameled on the back with the same pattern as the set itself. Coffee sets mirrored the latest styles far more than the traditional tea sets, and there are examples of Art Nouveau patterns, Art Deco patterns, and even some very simple modern patterns. Coffee sets, especially top quality examples, were often hand painted and gilded and were decorated with full landscape patterns. These sets are among the most sought after and popular collectors' items.

Nice example of a highly decorated teacup and saucer with internal and external decoration and pedestal form. Blue mark. Good condition. £100/120. $145/175.

Tea sets didn't take on the modern form and content until the late 1940s and early 1950s when a set always came with a large teapot, and the normal size for the set was a six place setting rather than a twelve place set. Patterns and styling were far more simple and the decoration, if any, was more likely to be transfer printed than hand painted.

Example of a typical later trio with transfer print decoration. Red mark. Perfect condition. £30/40. $45/60.

Chocolate sets, which would normally comprise a tall chocolate pot and six tall cups on saucers, were not terribly popular in Europe, being much more accepted in America where hot chocolate was a far more popular social beverage. Very few chocolate sets were available in Europe, and most examples of complete sets are generally American export sets that have come to England via the United States.

In addition to the boxed sets already mentioned, there are some variations to the standard sets. The breakfast set is often mistaken for an incomplete tea set, and comprises of a teapot, milk jug, sugar bowl, two cups and saucers, and ONE biscuit plate. The set was sold with these components and is a complete set. Cabaret or tray sets are the other variant and this can be either for tea or coffee, but the complement is similar. There should be a teapot or coffee pot, milk/cream jug, sugar bowl, and EITHER one or two cups and saucers. These components all stand on a round or oval tray.

Tea and coffee sets provide probably the most collected pieces made by Noritake. Complete sets are fairly rare and command a premium, as do the much rarer cabaret sets; however, teacups and saucers or trios (cup, saucer, and sideplate) are readily available as individual items, as are individual coffee cups and saucers. Coffee cans and saucers, especially the very decorative examples, are the most popular of the individual pieces. A word of caution: although it would appear to be an easy exercise to collect component parts with the intention of completing a tea or coffee set, it tends to be a virtually impossible task as the diverse range of mold shape and pattern combinations, along with the fact that many collectors just collect individual items, make completing a set an improbable proposition. Once again, as these were designed as utility wares, be careful to check for damage, but look out for the highly decorated cabinet examples, especially pedestal cups and saucers.

Simple trio with gilding. Blue mark. Perfect. £40/50. $60/70.

Trio with hexagonal cup and saucer and round plate. Blue mark. Perfect. £75/85. $110/120.

Trio with pedestal form cup. Blue mark. Perfect. £90/110. $125/150.

Trio with internal decoration to cup. Blue mark. Perfect. £90/100. $125/145.

Trio with hexagonal cup and saucer and round plate. Blue mark. Good. £75/85. $110/120.

Floral cup and saucer. Green mark. Perfect. £40/60. $60/85.

Floral trio. Green mark. Perfect. £40/60. $60/85.

Trio with internal decoration to cup. Blue mark. Good. £60/80. $85/115.

Fluted trio. Blue mark. Perfect. £40/50. $60/70.

Trio with round cup and saucer and square plate. Blue mark. Perfect. £30/40. $45/60.

Good hexagonal cup and saucer with internal decoration to the cup. Blue mark. Perfect. £90/110. $125/150.

Good trio with internal decoration. Blue mark. Perfect. £120/140. $175/210.

Fluted cup and saucer. Blue mark. Perfect. £110/130. $160/190.

Well decorated cabinet trio of semi-pedestal form. Blue mark. Perfect. £160/180. $230/260.

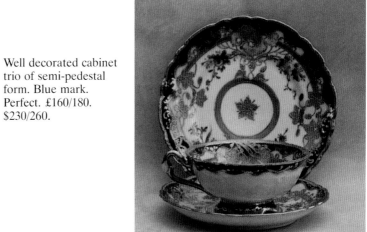

Another view of previous trio to show internal decoration.

Very decorative miniature cabinet cup and saucer. Blue mark. Perfect. £160/180. $220/250.

Far left: Cabinet trio of semi-pedestal form. Blue mark. Perfect. £140/160. $210/230.

Left: Another view of previous trio to show internal decoration.

Pedestal cup and saucer. Blue mark. Perfect. £110/130. $160/190.

Early jewelled trio of semi-pedestal form. Komaru mark. Perfect. £100/120. $145/175.

Another view of the pedestal cup and saucer to show decoration and backstamp.

Another view to show external decoration.

Unusual shape cup and saucer, could be for tea or coffee. Komaru mark. Good. £50/60. $70/85.

Semi-pedestal form scenic trio. Blue mark. Perfect. £30/40. $45/60.

Trio in Orange Desert Scene. Blue mark. Good. £30/40. $45/60.

Scenic cup and saucer. Blue mark. Perfect. £70/80. $100/115.

Good trio of semi-pedestal form in Pheasant pattern. Blue mark. Perfect. £160/180. $225/250.

Good cup and saucer in Desert Scene. Blue mark. Perfect. £120/140. $175/210.

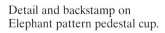

Detail and backstamp on Elephant pattern pedestal cup.

Good cup and saucer in Desert Scene of pedestal form. Blue mark. Perfect. £160/180. $230/260.

Very rare pedestal form cup and saucer in Elephant pattern. Green mark. Perfect. £220/250. $320/360.

Cup and saucer in Geisha Girl scene.
Green mark. Good. £40/50. $60/70.

Unusual moriageware child's cup and saucer.
Blue mark. Cup 2" high, saucer 3.5" dia. Good.
£70/80. $100/115.

Milk and sugar. Blue mark. Milk 3.5" high. Good. £65/85. £90/120.

Milk and sugar. Red mark. Milk
3.5" high. Perfect. £50/70. $70/100.

Milk and sugar. Red mark. Milk
3.5" high. Perfect. £50/70. $70/100.

Cream and sugar. Red mark. Cream
3" high. Perfect. £75/95. $110/130.

Milk and sugar. Blue mark.
Milk 3.5" high. Perfect.
£75/95. $110/130.

Cream and sugar. Blue mark. Milk
3" high. Perfect. £50/60. $70/85.

Cream and covered sugar in
Geisha Girl pattern. Green
mark. Cream 3.25" high, sugar
3.5" high. Perfect. £95/110.
$135/160.

Good scenic cream and sugar.
Blue mark. Perfect. £160/185.
$230/265.

Good milk and sugar in Desert
Scene. Blue mark. Milk 3.5" high.
Perfect. £160/185. $230/265.

Scenic cream and sugar.
Green mark. Good. £70/90.
$100/125.

Good cream and sugar in Desert Scene. Blue mark. Perfect. £225/250. $325/375.

Good cream and sugar in Desert Scene, from a strawberry set. Blue mark. Cream 3" high. Perfect. £220/235. $290/325.

Unusual pattern cream and sugar. Red mark. Perfect. £75/95. $110/135.

Later transfer printed cream jug. Red mark.
Good. £50/60. $70/85.

Early milk jug. Komaru mark. 3.75" high. Perfect. £75/95. $110/135.

Milk jug. Blue mark. 3"
high. Perfect. £75/95.
$110/135.

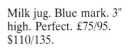

Cream jug. Green mark. Perfect. £65/70.
$90/100.

Good floral cream jug. Blue mark. Perfect.
£65/85. 90/120.

Early pedestal milk jug. Komaru mark. 4.5" high.
Perfect. £125/150. $180/220.

Well gilded semi-pedestal milk jug.
Blue mark. 3.75" high. Perfect.
£175/195. $250/270.

Scenic cream jug. Blue mark. 3" high. Perfect.
£50/70. $70/100.

Milk jug in Orange Desert Scene. Green
mark. 3.5" high. Good. £35/45. $50/65.

Scenic cream jug in luster finish. Green mark.
Good. £55/65. $80/90.

Good scenic cream jug. Blue mark. Perfect.
£95/110. $135/160.

Good milk jug in Desert Scene. Blue mark. Perfect. £125/150. $180/220.

Hexagonal milk jug. Blue mark. 3.5" high. Perfect. £95/110. $135/160.

Cream jug. Red mark. Perfect. £55/75. $80/110.

Pedestal milk jug with crabstock handle. Blue mark. 5" high. Perfect. £100/125. $145/180.

Early miniature moriageware milk jug from child's tea set. Blue mark. 1.75" high. Good. £75/95. $110/135.

Good footed milk jug in matte finish with heavy gilding. Blue mark. 3.5" high. Perfect. £140/160. $210/230.

Good footed sugar basin and cover in matte finish with heavy gilding. Blue mark. 5" high, overall width 7". Perfect. £190/200. $265/290.

Slop bowl. Komaru mark. 6" dia. Good. £60/80. $85/115.

Good pedestal milk jug in Desert Scene. Blue mark. Perfect. £150/170. $220/250.

Slop bowl in Desert Scene. Blue mark. 5.5" dia. Good. £85/100. $120/145.

Covered sugar basin. Blue mark. 3" high. Good. £65/85. $90/120.

Covered sugar basin. Blue mark. 3.25"
high. Perfect. £75/95. $110/135.

Covered sugar basin. Blue mark. Perfect. £95/110. $135/160.

Covered sugar basin. Blue mark. 3" high. Perfect. £45/60.
$65/80.

Covered sugar basin. Green mark. Average. £45/60. $65/80.

Hexagonal form covered sugar basin. Blue mark. 3.25" high.
£120/150. $175/220.

Good pedestal form covered sugar
basin. Blue mark. 5.5" high. Perfect.
£160/185. $230/265.

Coffee can and saucer. Red mark. Can 2.25" high, 2.75"
overall width including handle, saucer 4.25" dia. Perfect.
£20/30. $30/45.

Good scenic pedestal form covered
sugar basin. Blue mark. Perfect.
£160/185. $230/265.

Coffee can and saucer. Red mark. Perfect. £20/30. $30/45.

Coffee can and saucer. Red mark. Perfect. £20/30. $30/45.

Coffee can and saucer. Red mark. Perfect. £20/30. $30/45.

Coffee can and saucer. Red mark. Perfect. £20/30. $30/45.

Coffee can and saucer. Red mark. Perfect. £20/30. $30/45.

Scenic coffee can and saucer. Red mark. Perfect. £20/30. $30/45.

Coffee can and saucer. Green mark. Perfect. £30/40.
$45/60.

Coffee can and saucer. Blue mark. Perfect. £30/40.
$45/60.

Coffee can and saucer. Green mark. Perfect.
£30/40. $45/60.

Coffee can and saucer. Blue mark. Perfect. £30/40. $45/60.

Coffee can and saucer. Blue mark. Perfect. £40/50.
$60/70.

Coffee can and saucer. Blue mark. Perfect. £40/50.
$60/70.

Coffee can and saucer. Blue mark. Good. £25/30. $35/45.

Miniature coffee can and saucer. Blue mark. Can 2" high, 2.25" wide overall including handle, saucer 4" dia. Perfect. £75/85. $110/120.

Coffee can and saucer. Blue mark. Perfect. £55/65. $80/90.

Coffee can and saucer in Elephant pattern. Green mark. Good. £120/140. $175/210.

Coffee can and saucer. Blue mark. Perfect. £40/50. $60/70.

Miniature coffee can and saucer. Blue mark. Good. £30/40. $45/60.

Miniature coffee can and saucer. Blue mark. Good. £45/55. $65/80.

Miniature coffee can and saucer. Blue mark. Good. £50/60. £70/85.

Coffee can and saucer. Blue mark. Good. £40/50. $60/70.

Coffee can and saucer. Blue mark. Good. £45/55. $65/80.

Miniature coffee can and saucer. Blue mark. Good £50/60. $70/85.

Scenic coffee can and saucer in luster glaze. Blue mark. Good £25/35. $35/50.

Coffee can and saucer. Blue mark. Good £35/45. $50/65.

Miniature coffee can and saucer. Blue mark. Perfect. £30/40. $45/60.

Coffee can and saucer. Blue mark. Good. £40/50. $60/70.

Coffee can and saucer. Blue mark. Good. £30/40. $45/60.

Miniature coffee can and saucer. Blue mark. Good. £35/45. $50/65.

Miniature coffee can and saucer in Geisha Girl pattern. Blue mark. Good. £35/45. $50/65.

Coffee can and saucer in luster glaze. Blue mark. Good. £35/45. $50/65.

Miniature scenic coffee can and saucer. Blue mark. Perfect. £70/80. $100/115.

Miniature scenic coffee can and saucer. Blue mark. Perfect. £75/85. $110/120.

Miniature scenic coffee can and saucer. Blue mark. Perfect. £75/85 $110/120.

Miniature coffee can and saucer in Desert Scene. Blue mark. Perfect. £85/95. $120/135.

Miniature scenic coffee can and saucer. Blue mark. Perfect. £85/95. $120/135.

Coffee can and saucer. Blue mark. Perfect. £35/45. $50/65.

Good miniature scenic coffee can and saucer. Blue mark. Perfect. £90/110. $125/150.

Scenic coffee can and saucer. Blue mark. Perfect. £75/85. $110/120.

Coffee can and saucer in Howo Bird pattern. Blue mark. Perfect. £30/40. $45/60.

Scenic coffee can and saucer. Blue mark. Perfect. £70/80. $110/115.

Scenic coffee can and saucer. Blue mark. Good. £70/80. $100/115.

Coffee can and saucer. Blue mark. Good. £30/40. $45/60.

Coffee can in Desert Scene with matching spoon, probably originally part of a boxed presentation set. Blue mark. Perfect. £110/130. $160/190.

Coffee can and saucer. Blue mark. Good. £30/40. $45/60.

Coffee can and saucer. Blue mark. Can 2.25" high, 2.75" overall width including handle, saucer 4.5" dia. Perfect. £25/35. $35/50.

Coffee can and saucer. Blue mark. Good. £25/35. $35/45.

Coffee can and saucer in a variation of Geisha Girl with better gilding, more detailed painting, and a matching enameled spoon. This was probably part of a presentation set, and illustrates the difference between a normal utility piece and a cabinet piece. Blue mark. Perfect. £100/120. $145/175.

Scenic coffee can and saucer with heavy gilding. Blue mark. Good. £70/80. $100/115.

Coffee can and saucer. Blue mark. Good. £55/65. $80/90.

Coffee can and saucer in Geisha Girl pattern. Blue mark. Perfect. £30/40. $45/60.

Scenic coffee can and saucer. Blue mark. Perfect. £70/80. $100/115.

Coffee cup and saucer. Green mark. Perfect. £25/35. $35/50.

Good coffee can and saucer, heavily gilded with matching enameled spoon. Probably from a presentation set. Blue mark. Perfect. £100/120. $145/175.

Coffee can and octagonal saucer. Green mark. Perfect. £50/60 $70/85.

Coffee cup and octagonal saucer. Green mark. Cup 2.25" high, overall width including handle 2.75", saucer 4.5" dia. Perfect. £25/35. $35/50.

Coffee cup and saucer. Red mark. Cup 2.25" high, 2.75" overall width including handle, saucer 4.5" dia. Perfect. £25/35. $35/50.

Coffee cup and saucer. Red mark. Perfect. £25/25. $35/50.

Coffee cup and saucer. Blue mark. Perfect. £35/45. $50/65.

Coffee cup and saucer. Green mark. Perfect. £25/35. $35/50.

Coffee cup and saucer. Red mark. Perfect. £25/35. $35/50.

Coffee cup and saucer. Blue mark. Perfect. £30/40. $45/60.

Coffee cup and saucer. Red mark. Perfect. £25/35. $35/50.

Coffee cup and saucer. Green mark. Perfect. £25/35. $35/50.

Coffee cup and saucer. Blue mark. Cup 2.25" high, 3.75" overall width including handle. Saucer 4.25" dia. Good. £60/70. $85/100.

Coffee cup and saucer. Green mark. Perfect. £25/35. $35/50.

Coffee can and saucer in Desert Scene, matte finish. Blue mark. Good. £90/110. $125/150.

Coffee cup and saucer. Red mark. Good. £25/35. $35/50.

Coffee pot. Green mark. 6.5" high. Perfect. £90/110. $125/150.

Coffee pot. Blue mark. 7" high. Perfect. £90/110. $125/150.

Coffee pot. Blue mark. 6.75" high. Perfect. £110/140. $160/210.

Coffee pot. Red mark. 7" high. Perfect. £60/85. $85/120.

Scenic coffee pot. Blue mark. 6.75" high. Perfect. £85/100. $120/145.

Scenic coffee pot. Blue mark. 6.75" high. Perfect. £220/250. $320/350.

Scenic coffee pot. Blue mark. 6.75" high. Perfect. £190/220. $265/320.

Scenic coffee pot with luster glaze. Green mark. 6.75" high. Perfect. £65/85. $90/120.

Pedestal coffee pot. Red mark. 7"
high. Perfect. £75/95. $110/135.

Good coffee pot in Desert Scene. Blue mark.
6.75" high. Perfect. £280/320. $400/450.

Teapot. Red mark. 6.5"
high. Perfect. £50/60.
$70/85.

Coffee pot, cream and sugar. Green mark. Pot 7" high. Perfect. £90/110. $125/160.

Coffee set. Red mark. Pot 6.75" high. Perfect. (Value for complete set with six coffee cans and saucers) £260/280. $365/395.

Coffee set. Red mark. Pot 6.75" high. Perfect. (Value for complete set with six coffee cans and saucers) £260/280. $365/395.

Coffee set. Red mark. Pot 6.75" high. Perfect. (Value for complete set with six coffee cans and saucers) £340/360. $475/500.

Coffee set. Red mark. Pot 6.75" high. Perfect. (Value for complete set with six coffee cans and saucers) £340/360. $475/500.

Coffee set. Red mark. Pot 7" high. Perfect. (Value for complete set with six coffee cups and saucers) £150/180. $220/260.

Coffee set in Geisha Girl pattern. Green mark. Pot 7" high. Perfect. (Value for complete set with six coffee cups and saucers) £400/450. $560/630.

Coffee set. Blue mark. Pot 7" high. Perfect. £250/300. $360/425.

Coffee set. Green mark. Pot 7.5" high. Good. (Value for complete set with six coffee cups and saucers) £250/300. $360/425.

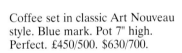

Coffee set in classic Art Nouveau style. Blue mark. Pot 7" high. Perfect. £450/500. $630/700.

Coffee set. Blue mark. Pot 6.5" high. Perfect. £500/550. $700/775.

Coffee set. Blue mark. Pot 6.75" high. Perfect. (Value for complete set with six coffee cans and saucers) £500/550. $700/775.

Coffee set in Desert Scene. Blue mark. Pot 6.75" high. Perfect. Set £1250/1350. $1750/2000.

Cabaret set. Blue mark. Pot 6.75" high, tray 12" dia. Good. £850/950. $1200/1350.

Very rare cabaret set in Desert Scene with matte finish. Blue mark. Perfect. £1700/2000. $2500/3000.

Pedestal teapot with crabstock handle. Blue mark. 6.75" high. Perfect. £200/220. $280/310.

Good scenic pedestal teapot with crabstock handle in very rare Elephant pattern. Green mark. 6.75" high. Perfect. £450/500. $630/700.

Good scenic pedestal teapot with crabstock handle. Blue mark. 6.75" high. Perfect. £300/350. $425/495.

Semi-pedestal teapot. Komaru mark. 4.5" high. Perfect. £220/250. $320/360.

Teapot, milk, and covered
sugar. Blue mark. Teapot 6"
high. Perfect. £500/550.
$700/770.

Teapot, milk, and covered
sugar. Blue mark. Teapot
6" high. Perfect. £550/600.
$775/850.

Scenic teapot, milk, and
covered sugar. Blue mark.
Teapot 5" high. Perfect.
£350/400. $495/560.

Tea set of squat form. Blue mark. Teapot 5" high. Perfect. Price
for complete set with six cups and saucers. £700/800. $1000/1150.

Good set of pedestal teapot, milk, and covered sugar in Desert Scene. Blue mark. Teapot 6.75" high. Perfect.
£700/750. $1000/1100.

Highly decorative tea set of fluted form in a rare mold shape. Blue mark. Perfect. £900/1000. $1250/1400.

Cabinet tea set of pedestal form with heavy gilding. Blue mark. Teapot 6.75" high. Perfect. Set £650/700. $900/1000.

Cabinet tea set of pedestal form. Blue mark. Teapot 6.75" high. Perfect.(Value for complete set with four pedestal cups and saucers) £850/900. $1150/1250.

Good pedestal tea set in Desert Scene. Blue mark. Teapot 6.75" high. Perfect. (Value for complete tea set with four pedestal cups and saucers) £1400/1500. $1950/2100.

Very rare pedestal tea set in Elephant pattern. Green mark. Teapot 6.75" high. Perfect. (Value for complete tea set with four pedestal cups and saucers) £2000/2200. $2800/3200.

Detail from Elephant pattern tea set showing gilding and jewelling.

Presentation coffee set in original box. Blue mark. Perfect. £700/750. $1000/1100.

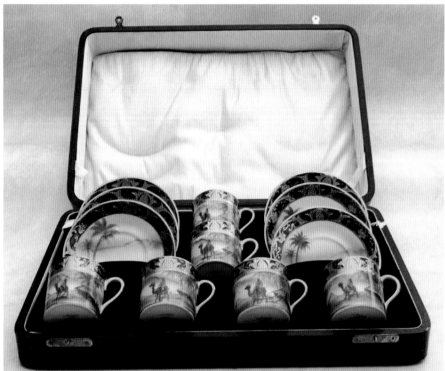

Presentation coffee set in Desert Scene in original box. Blue mark. Perfect. £800/900. $1150/1250.

Presentation coffee set with silver spoons in original box. Green mark. Perfect. £850/950. $1200/1300.

Chapter Nine

Vases

Vases have always been the most popular of fancies produced by any manufacturer. Although the specific use for a vase is simply as a form of holder for a floral or decorative display, the holder itself has become collectible in its own right. The body of a vase has provided a wonderful canvas for the painter, decorator, and gilder to demonstrate their skills and some of the best work produced by the Noritake Company has been illustrated on their vases.

There are three basic styles of vase shown in this book. The most common type is the "normal" open-mouthed vase that conforms to the usual perception of the vase shape, and would have been used as our basic display holder. There are, of course, infinite variations of this type of vase in terms of shape and size. Those vases designed for a specific use, such as a narrow-necked example commonly termed a bud vase, which should hold just a single flower, or a squat globular shape commonly termed a posy vase, which would be used for a display of very small stemmed flowers.

There are illustrated examples of the "bolted urn" style of vase. This style, so called because it is normally made in three separate parts which are all joined by a single bolt connector: the base, which is normally a single foot and can be square, cuboid, hexagonal, or even round in shape, a small stem, which sits between the base and the body, and the urn-shaped body itself. These bolted urns generally also have covers, making the whole assembly a four part piece; although, there are examples of three piece bolted urns, which, from the style of top rim decoration, would not have had a cover.

The third style of vase is not really a vase, by the strictest definition, but is usually called a "Temple Jar" in Europe, although in America it is simply referred to as a "covered urn." A temple jar is a form of vase that generally has a clean ovoid body, with no handles, and a flanged cover with a large knop. This style can range from an almost globular shape of approximately 4 inches in height up to a huge 15 inches or bigger, but all are definite ovoids with covers. Just to make life interesting, there is a variation on the temple jar which is of the same basic form, however the lid is a simple half hemisphere that has no knop. This is normally termed a "Ginger Jar." There are very few examples of ginger jars from Noritake, but there is one illustrated later.

Vase style and pattern very much reflects the period of manufacture from the earliest Moriageware examples illustrating Majolica-like form and decoration through simplistic Arts and Crafts styles into Heavy Victorian decoration and gilding. The later examples illustrate Art Nouveau style with echoes of William Morris inspired design and then there are the Art Deco styles and shapes with Luster glazes and bright colors. The later vases illustrated carry the far simpler floral designs and motifs popularized in the mid to late 1930s by English manufacturers such as Shelly and Carlton.

The style of decoration also runs the full spectrum of possibilities, from very simple transfer prints to heavy and intricate gilding with beading and jeweling with hand-painted scenic cartouches in gilt frames. The range of ground colors is almost infinite, and the most popular is probably cobalt blue, although there are many examples in light blue, red, pink, yellow, green, and white. The ground colors tend to reflect the output of the bigger European manufacturers, Cobalt being very popular with Coalport and Derby, while the lighter blues and pinks tend to mirror those used extensively by Minton. The greens and yellows are similar to the grounds popular with Sevres and the German factories and the white grounds were, of course, universal.

Vases were among the most favorite items bought as decorative pieces as most houses of the period had large mantelpieces over open fires and sideboards were a standard furnishing item. Vases were the ideal form of ornamental decoration for these areas and therefore extremely popular. The demand was for pairs of vases, which was at odds with the traditional Japanese custom of displaying a single vase as a decorative item. Vases in pairs were produced to meet this demand, and the decoration on the majority of each pair was mirrored, that is, applied so that the pattern was reversed on one vase from the other. This made a superb decorative effect when the pair was set at either end of the mantelpiece or sideboard, and could be further enhanced by obtaining a garniture. A garniture in this form is a set of three items all in the same basic pattern, and a typical garniture might be a pair of vases with a centerpiece (which is a vase of a different shape, or a bolted urn, or even a temple jar). The style was a development of the classic continental garniture, which normally had a clock as the centerpiece.

For collectors, vases are very popular provided there is somewhere to display them properly. Vases can be among the most expensive items as a top quality mirrored pair in a scenic pattern can demand in excess of £1000 ($1400); however, there are plenty of small individual vases available from around £30 ($45). Condition is always important with vases. By virtue of their original use, they are more prone to wear on the gilding from dusting, and many are damaged. Look out for restoration on vases, especially on the handles and upper rims. Look for refixed knops on temple jar covers and this also applies to bolted urns if they have covers. The rims of the covers themselves are also prone to damage, so check them carefully.

Miniature floral vase. Blue mark. Perfect. 2.5" high. £30/35. $40/50.

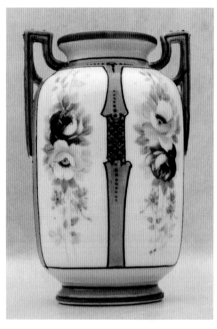

Miniature floral vase. Blue mark. Perfect. 2.5" high. £25/30. $35/45.

Miniature landscape vase. Green mark. Good. 2.5" high. £15/20. $20/30.

Miniature floral vase. Blue mark. Perfect. 2.5" high. £25/30. $35/45.

Miniature landscape vase. Blue mark. Perfect. 2.5" high. £30/45. $40/50.

Minature luster landscape vase. Green mark. Good. 3" high. £20/25. $30/45.

Miniature luster landscape vase. Blue mark. Good. 4" high. £35/40. $50/60.

Miniature luster landscape vase. Blue mark. Good. 3" high. £25/30. $35/45.

Desert Scene vase. Blue mark. Good. 14" high. £250/300. $360/425.

Miniature luster landscape vase. Blue mark. Good. 3" high. £25/30. $35/45.

Scenic vase. Blue mark. Perfect. 6.5"
high. £110/130. $160/190.

Scenic vase. Blue mark. Good. 5.5" high.
£110/130. $160/190.

Floral vase. Blue mark. Good. 11" high. £250/300. $360/425.

Floral vase. Blue mark. Good. 4.25" high. £110/130.
$160/190.

Scenic vase. Blue mark. Good. 5.5" high. £120/140.
$175/210.

Scenic vase. Blue mark. Good. 6.5" high.
£200/240. $290/350.

Scenic vase. Blue mark. Good. 5.5" high. £100/120.
$145/175.

Heavily jewelled and gilded vase. Komaru
mark. Good. 7.5" high. £250/300. $360/425.

Desert Scene vase. Blue mark. Good. 5.5"
high. £200/240. $290/350.

Three handled scenic vase. Blue mark.
Good. 4.5" high. £40/50. $60/70.

Ornate two handled vase with heavy decoration. Blue mark.
7" high x 7" overall width. Perfect. £275/300. $400/425.

Scenic vase. Blue mark. Good. 5" high. £100/120. $145/175.

Scenic vase. Blue mark. Good. 8" high. £100/120. $145/175.

Floral vase. Blue mark. Good. 6" high. £150/180. $220/260.

Desert Scene vase. Blue mark. Perfect. 10.5" high. £650/700. $900/1000.

Floral vase. Blue mark. Good. 7" high.
£120/150. $175/220.

Desert Scene vase. Blue mark. 5.75" high. Perfect.
£300/325. $425/460.

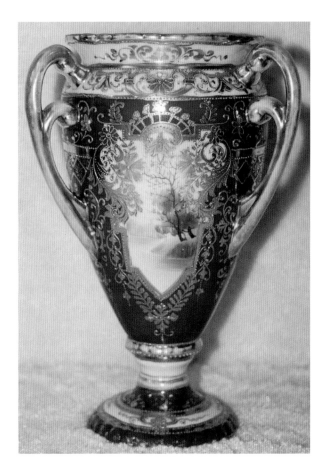

Three handled scenic vase. Blue mark. Good. 8.25" high.
£180/220. $260/320.

Desert Scene vase. Blue mark.
Good. 6.5" high. £350/400. $495/550.

Desert Scene vase. Matte finish. Blue mark. Perfect.
5.5" high. £220/250. $320/360.

Scenic vase. Blue mark. Perfect. 5.5" high.
£225/250. $325/360.

Desert Scene vase. Blue mark. Good.
3.5" high. £150/175. $220/250.

Vase with seahorse handles. Blue mark. Perfect. 8.5" high.
£250/300. $360/425.

Floral vase. Blue mark. Good. 8" high. £120/150. $175/220.

Scenic vase. Blue mark. Good. 5.5" high. £80/100. $115/145.

Picture vase. Blue mark. Good. 5.5" high. £80/100. $115/145.

Scenic vase. Blue mark. Perfect. 11" high. £180/220. $260/320.

Scenic vase. Blue mark. Good.
11" high. £150/180. $220/260.

Scenic vase. Blue mark.
Good. 10" high. £125/150.
$180/220.

Heavily gilded vase. Blue
mark. Good. 9" high.
£175/225. $250/300.

Floral vase. Blue mark. Perfect. 9" high. £250/300. $360/425.

Squat landscape
vase. Blue mark.
Good. 3.5" high.
£100/120. $145/175.

Squat bottle vase. Blue mark. Perfect. 3.5" high. £140/160.
$210/230.

Bottle vase. Komaru
mark. Good. 6.5"
high. £120/150.
$175/220.

Squat bottle vase.
Blue mark. Good.
3.5" high. £120/150.
$175/220.

Squat bottle vase in Desert Scene. Blue mark. Good. 3.5" high.
£250/300. $360/425.

Vase in Elephant pattern. Rare. Green mark.
Good. 6.5" high. £275/325. $400/460.

Ginger jar. Rare shape. Blue mark. Good. 7.25" high. £200/250.
$290/360.

Closer view of painting detail on Elephant pattern vase.

Temple jar and cover.
Blue mark. Good. 10"
high. £275/300. $400/450.

Temple jar and cover. Blue
mark. Perfect. 6.5" high.
£300/350. $425/500.

Temple jar & cover. Blue mark. Good.
6.5" high. £225/275. $325/400.

Covered jar. Blue
mark. Good. 6.5"
high. £225/275.
$325/400.

Temple jar and cover. Blue mark. Good.
10" high. £250/300. $360/425.

Temple jar and cover in Desert Scene. Blue mark. Good. 6.5" high. £400/450. $560/630.

Bolted urn and cover. Green mark. Perfect. 13" high. £500/600. $700/850.

Temple jar and cover, heavily jewelled and gilded. Shipping Scene. Rare. Blue mark. Perfect. 8" high. £900/1100. $1250/1550.

Rear of Shipping Scene temple jar showing continuous pattern.

Bolted urn and cover. Blue mark. Perfect.
10" high. £300/350. $425/500.

Closer view of the painting and jewelling detail on the Shipping Scene bolted urn.

Bolted urn and cover. Blue
mark. Perfect. 8.75" high.
£300/350. $425/500.

Bolted urn and cover, heavily jewelled and
gilded. Shipping Scene. Rare. Blue mark.
15" high. Perfect. £900/1100. $1250/1550.

114

Pair of miniature luster vases. Green mark. 3" high. Good.
£30/40. $45/60.

Mirrored pair of miniature vases. Blue mark. 3" high. Good.
£45/60. $65/85.

Pair of miniature luster vases. Green mark. 3" high. Good.
£30/40. $45/60.

Pair of scenic vases. Blue mark. 5" high. Good. £40/60. $60/80

Pair of miniature luster vases. Green mark. 3" high. Good.
£30/40. $45/60

Pair of three handled floral vases. Blue mark. 4.5" high. Good.
£60/80. $85/115

115

Mirrored pair of matte vases with moriage finish. Blue mark. 6.25" high. Good. £60/80. $85/115.

Pair of floral vases with moriage finish. Blue mark. 5" high. Good. £70/80. $100/120.

Pair of floral vases with moriage finish. Blue mark. 4" high. Good. £125/150. $180/220.

Good pair of floral vases. Blue mark. 6.5" high. Perfect. £325/375. $460/525.

Mirrored pair of floral vases. Blue mark. 7.5" high. Average. £200/250. $290/360.

Mirrored pair of Dragon vases. Blue mark. 11" high. Good. £250/300. $360/425.

Good pair of floral vases. Blue
mark. 4.25" high. Perfect.
£250/280. $360/410.

Mirrored pair of scenic vases. Blue mark.
7.5" high. Good. £300/350. $425/500.

Pair of Geisha Girl vases. Blue mark.
7.5" high. Average. £140/160.
$210/230.

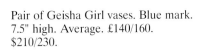

Mirrored pair of floral vases. Blue mark. 5.5"
high. Perfect. £350/400. $495/560.

Mirrored pair of vases in Desert Scene. Blue mark.
8.5" high. Perfect. £700/800. $1000/1150.

Good mirrored pair of scenic vases. Blue mark.
12" high. Perfect. £500/600. $700/850.

Pair of scenic vases with unusual ram figured feet. Blue mark. 7.5" high. Perfect. £500/600. $700/850.

Mirrored pair of squat bottle vases. Blue mark. 3.5" high. Good. £250/300. $360/425.

Mirrored pair of squat bottle vases. Blue mark. 3.5" high. Good. £240/260. $350/375.

Good pair of squat bottle vases in Desert Scene. Blue mark. 3.5" high. Perfect. £450/550. $630/770.

Pair of stylized floral vases. Blue mark. 4.5" high. Good. £280/320. $400/450.

Good pair of mirrored vases in Desert Scene. Blue mark. 8.5" high. Perfect. £750/850. $1100/1200.

121

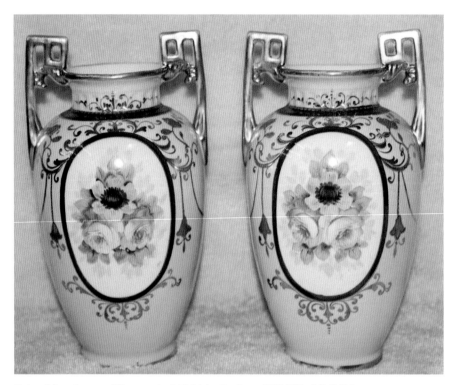

Pair of floral vases. Blue mark. 5.5" high. Perfect. £300/350. $425/495.

Pair of floral vases on Cobalt ground. Blue mark. 5.5" high. Good. £450/500. $630/700.

Mirrored pair of floral vases with scenic cartouches. Blue mark. 5.5" high. Good.
£350/400. $495/560.

Closer look at landscape paintwork detail on floral/scenic pair.

Rare mirrored pair of vases with Shipping Scene. Blue mark. 8" high. Good. £700/900. $1000/1250.

Mirrored pair of scenic vases. Blue mark. 4.5" high. Good. £200/250. $290/360.

Pair of floral vases. Blue mark. 9.5" high. Good. £250/300. $360/425.

Pair of floral vases. Blue mark. 9.5" high. Good. £220/250. $320/360.

Pair of floral vases. Blue mark. 5.5" high. Good. £150/200. $220/290.

Mirrored pair of vases with stylized exotic birds. Blue mark. 9" high. Good. £220/250. $320/360.

Pair of floral vases. Green mark. 11" high. Good. £180/220. $260/320.

Pair of floral vases. Blue mark. 10" high. Good. £350/450. $495/630.

Very good pair of heavily gilded floral vases. Blue mark. 6" high. Perfect. £800/900. $1150/1250.

Pair of scenic vases. Blue mark. 5" high.
Good. £250/300. $360/425.

Pair of gilded floral vases. Blue mark.
6.5" high. Perfect. £380/420. $530/590.

Good pair of vases, Arab dhows on cobalt
ground. Blue mark. 6.5" high. Perfect.
£480/520. $675/735.

Pair of floral vases on cream ground. Blue mark. 9.25" high. Good. £350/400. $495/560

Mirrored pair of scenic vases. Blue mark. 6.5" high. Good. £300/350. $425/495.

Mirrored pair of vases in Desert Scene. Blue mark. 5" high. Average. £240/260. $350/375.

Good mirrored pair of vases in Desert
Scene. Blue mark. 8" high. Perfect. £750/800.
$1100/1150.

Mirrored pair of vases in Desert Scene. Blue
mark. 8" high. Average. £200/220. $290/325.

Mirrored pair of vases in Desert Scene.
Blue mark. 14" high. Good. £800/1000.
$1150/1400.

Pair of floral vases. Blue mark. 8" high. Good. £450/500. $630/700.

Pair of floral vases. Blue mark. 8" high. Good. £450/500. $630/700.

Mirrored pair of scenic vases. Blue mark. 7.75" high. Good. £350/400. $500/550.

Very good mirrored pair of vases in Desert Scene. Blue mark. 8" high. Perfect. £900/1100. $1250/1550.

Mirrored pair of scenic vases in matte finish. Blue mark. Perfect. 6.25" high. £380/420. $540/590.

Good pair of three handled squat moriage vases. Komaru mark. 6" high. Good. £500/600. $700/850.

Rear view of pair of moriage vases showing continuous decoration.

Very rare mirrored pair of vases in Elephant Scene. Green mark. 6.5" high. Good. £600/700. $850/1000.

Mirrored pair of scenic bolted urns. Blue mark. 9" high. Good. £350/450. $495/625.

Mirrored pair of bolted urns and covers in Desert Scene. Blue mark. 12" high. Good. £900/1100. $1250/1450.

Mirrored pair of scenic vases. Blue mark. 12" high. Good. £700/900. $1000/1250.

Mirrored pair of floral bolted urns and covers. Komaru mark. 13" high. Good. £800/1000. $1150/1400.

Mirrored pair of scenic bolted urns and covers. 7" high. Good. £500/600. $700/850.

Mirrored pair of scenic bolted urns and covers. Blue mark. 9" high. £900/1100. $1250/1500.

Mirrored pair of bolted urns and covers in Desert Scene. Rare matte finish. Blue mark. 9" high. Good. £1000/1200. $1400/1700.

Pair of floral bolted urns and covers. Blue mark. 9" high. Good. £900/1100. $1250/1500.

Mirrored pair of scenic jars and covers of hexagonal form. Blue mark. 6.5" high Good.
£400/500. $560/700.

Pair of floral temple jars and covers. Blue mark. 6.5" high. Good. £600/700. $850/1000.

Mirrored pair of scenic temple jars and covers. Left jar turned to show reverse. Blue mark. 6.5" high. Good. £650/750. $900/1100.

Mirrored pair of temple jars and covers in Desert Scene. Blue mark. 10" high. Good. £900/1100. $1250/1500.

Very rare mirrored pair of temple jars and covers. Swans on a matte finish. Blue mark. 6.5" high. Good. £1000/1200. $1400/1700.

Fine mirrored pair of bolted urns and covers in Desert Scene of very rare form. Blue mark. 10.75" high. Perfect. £1600/1800. $2250/2500.

Chapter Ten

Dishes and Bowls

There are an infinite variety of dishes and bowls manufactured by Noritake. In many cases, individual bowls started life as part of a set, but are individually collectible. Among the sets manufactured by Noritake which included bowls are the fruit or berry set, which would comprise a 9 inch bowl, and six smaller bowls around 5 inches in diameter, and the celery set, which would have a large oblong dish, usually around 10 to 11 inches in length and six individual salt dishes. These salts could be in one of several shapes, the most common being a 4 inch oval, but there are several variations.

Bowls, generally, were manufactured for a specific use or function, although once in use, the original purpose became a little academic, and bowls simply provided a convenient receptacle for that particular moment. The main types of bowl, and their original intended uses are as follows:

Relish Dish

There were two main shapes for relish dishes, an oval around eight inches in length, and a similar shape and size with a handle at each end. These dishes could be single compartment or double compartment, and were used for relishes and pickles.

Relish dish. Blue mark. 8" dia. Good. £60/80. $85/115.

Salad Bowl

A salad bowl was usually round or hexagonal, and 9 inches in diameter, commonly with fluted sides and a flat base. Sometimes this was sold as part of a salad set, accompanied by six 5-inch shallow round bowls, which may have small handles.

Salad Bowl. Blue mark. 9.5" dia. Perfect. £330/360. $475/525.

Bonbon Dish

Bonbon dishes were designed to sit on the dining table containing mints or other sweets. These bonbon dishes could be octagonal or round and usually 7 inches in diameter. The dishes could have a fitted handle or be in an EPNS stand.

Bonbon dish. Blue mark. 7.5" dia. Perfect. £180/200. $260/290.

Fresh Fruit Bowl

Again, designed for the dining table, a fruit bowl was generally bigger than a salad bowl, 10 inches or more in diameter, and often had an EPNS rim.

Fruit bowl in Desert Scene. Blue mark. 10.5" dia. Perfect. £380/420. $550/600.

Lemon Dish

Lemon tea was very popular in the early years of the twentieth century and special dishes were designed to carry lemon slices. A lemon dish looked like a large saucer, around 6 inches in diameter, with either a loop handle on the side or a central pillar handle to enable the dish to be passed around.

Lemon dish. Red mark. 6.5" dia. Perfect. £30/40. $45/60.

Mayonnaise Set

A complete mayonnaise set would comprise a small circular bowl, usually around four or five inches in diameter by three inches deep, standing on a matching saucer with a small ladle. All too often, the saucer and ladle are lost, but the mayonnaise bowl is easily identified by its three ball feet.

Mayonnaise ladle. Blue mark. 4" long. Perfect. £35/45. $55/65.

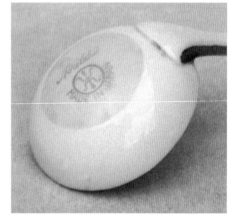

Underside of mayonnaise ladle to show backstamp.

Mayonnaise dish. Blue mark. 5.25" dia. Perfect. £90/110. $125/160.

Butter Dish

A butter dish is round, four or five inches in diameter by 3 inches deep, with two square handles that are part of the sides, and molded vertically instead of horizontally like most handles. This also should be a three part dish with a cover which is round with two cut-outs which fit around the vertical handles and a pierced insert which sits in the base of the dish. Sadly, butter dishes complete with the base insert are very rare indeed, as this small flat perforated plate is usually lost. Butter dishes would normally be complete with an EPNS stand, another part of the original set that is often missing.

Butter dish with cover, but missing the insert. Blue mark. Dish 5" dia. Good. £60/80. $85/115.

Nut Set

Nut sets were popular in America, where the set consisted of a large bowl, 6 or 7 inches in diameter, accompanied by six smaller bowls of 3-inch diameter. Usually the nut set was in "Blow Out" form with hand painted fruit and nut decoration. They are a rarity in Europe, and the examples found generally have American Export backstamps.

Snack Dish

Snack dishes, which would contain small savories to be handed around at cocktail parties, were very common in the 1920s and 1930s. These highly decorative dishes were produced in a wide variety of forms and designs, but were usually compartmented, and had a handle for passing around. Quite often, the handle was a decorative highlight and would be figural in form.

Good example of a snack dish with a figural handle. Blue mark. 8.5" dia. Perfect. £150/170. $220/250.

Metal Frames or Stands

It was a regular practice to "enhance" the appearance of tablewares with metal rims or stands. In some rare occasions this was done with silver. If this to be the case, then usually the porcelain element was manufactured in Japan, and the piece was then fitted with the silver embellishment in England.

Example of a cake plate on an EPNS (Electro-Plated Nickel Silver) stand. Blue mark. 10" dia. Perfect. £40/50. $60/70.

In most pieces, the work was done using EPNS, which is Electro-Plated Nickel Silver. EPNS is a form of silver-plate which has good wear resistant properties and cleans in a similar fashion to silver, but is a lot cheaper to use. The common practice was to use EPNS for bowl rims, tazza stands, cake stands, and also to form a framework that the porcelain element fits inside. This can be found in cruet set stands and also stands for a cream and sugar set used with fresh soft fruits like strawberries or raspberries.

Good example of a strawberry set in a scenic design with an EPNS stand. Blue mark. Jug 3" high. Perfect. £240/260. $350/375.

Bowls and dishes, generally, are not the most popular collectible items because of the problems of display, however a good number of bowls and dishes were also decorated as cabinet pieces, with heavy gilding and intricate patterning. These cabinet pieces are very collectible and comparatively rare, especially if in perfect condition. Cabinet pieces are usually free from damage, but prone to wear on the gilding; however, the normal utility items should be checked carefully for damage as the majority of these wares were in everyday use.

Bowl. Blue mark. 4.5" dia. Good. £50/60. $70/85.

Bowl. Blue mark. 5.25" dia. Perfect. £20/30. $30/45.

Bowl. Blue mark. 5.5" dia. Good. £20/30. $30/45.

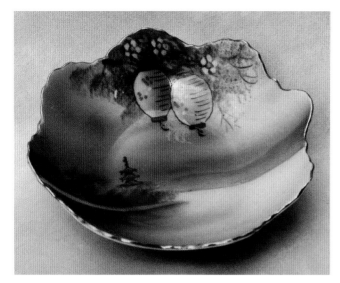

Bowl. Blue mark. 5.5" dia. Good. £30/40. $45/60.

Bowl with luster glaze. Blue mark. 5" dia. Good. £30/40. $45/60.

Bowl. Blue mark. 4.5" dia. Good. £20/30. $30/45.

Relish dish. Blue mark. 8.5" dia. Perfect. £80/100. $115/145.

Bowl with luster glaze. Blue mark. 5.5" dia. Good. £20/30. $30/45.

Bowl with luster glaze. Blue mark. 4.5" dia. Good. £20/30. $30/45.

143

Bowl. Blue mark. 7.5" dia. Good.
£80/100. $115/145.

Bowl. Blue mark. 9.5" dia. Good.
£50/60. $70/85.

Bowl. Blue mark. 9.5" dia. Perfect.
£50/60. $70/85.

Bowl. Blue mark. 4.5" dia. Good.
£20/30. $30/45.

Bowl in Geisha Girl pattern. Blue mark. 8.75" dia. Perfect. £70/80. $100/115.

Bowl. Blue mark. 8.75" dia. Perfect. £70/80. $100/115.

Good bowl with heavy gilding. Blue mark. 7.5" dia. Perfect. £180/200. $260/290.

145

Bowl. Blue mark. 6.5" dia. Perfect.
£120/130. $175/200.

Bowl. Blue mark. 7.5" dia. Perfect.
£80/100. $115/145.

Bowl with scenic cartouches. Blue mark. 4.5" dia.
Good. £50/60. $70/85.

Bowl. Blue mark. 7.5" dia. Perfect. £120/140. $175/210.

146

Bonbon dish. Blue mark. 8.75" dia. Good. £140/160. $210/230.

Fine dish in rare scenic pattern and heavy gilding. Blue mark. 9.25" dia. Perfect. £220/240. $320/350.

Good bowl with heavy gilding. Blue mark. 7.5" dia. Perfect. £160/180. $230/260.

Bowl. Green mark. 7.25" dia. Perfect. £120/130. $175/190.

Scenic bowl. Blue mark. 5.5" dia.
Good. £140/160. $210/230.

Good scenic bowl with heavy gilding. Blue
mark. 10.5" dia. Perfect. £280/300. $400/425.

Good dish in Desert Scene. Blue
mark. 10.5" dia. Perfect. £280/
300. $400/425.

Mayonnaise bowl in Desert Scene with matte finish. Blue mark. 4.25" dia. Perfect. £140/150. $210/225.

Dish in Desert Scene. Blue mark. 8.5" dia. Perfect. £140/160. $210/230.

Bowl in Desert Scene. Blue mark. 8" dia. Good. £160/180. $230/260.

Another view of the Desert Scene dish to show shape.

Bowl in Desert Scene. Blue mark. 5.5" dia. Perfect. £120/130. $175/190.

Bowl in Desert Scene. Blue mark. 6.75" dia. Good. £160/180. $230/260.

Mayonnaise dish in Desert Scene. Blue mark. 5.25" dia. Perfect. £150/170. $220/245.

Good relish bowl. Blue mark. 9.5" dia. Perfect. £140/160. $210/230.

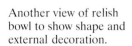

Another view of relish bowl to show shape and external decoration.

Relish bowl. Blue mark.
8.5" dia. Perfect. £140/160.
$210/230.

Snack dish. Blue mark. 7.75" dia.
Perfect. £90/110. $125/150.

Octagonal sweetmeat dish with moriage trim. Blue mark. 6.5" dia. Good.
£80/100. $115/145.

Individual salt dish, from celery set. Blue mark. 2.25" dia.
Perfect. £15/20. $20/30.

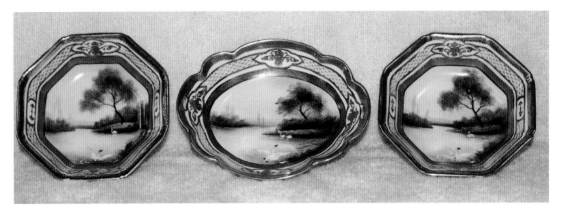

Set of three scenic bowls. Blue mark. Octagonal, 4.5" dia., oval 5.5" dia. Perfect. Set £300/320. $425/450.

Pin tray. Blue mark. 4.25" dia. Good. £45/55. $65/80.

Salad bowl. Blue mark. 9.5" dia. Good. £240/260. $350/375.

Bowl. Red mark. 6.5" dia. Good. £30/40. $45/60.

Octagonal scenic bowl. Blue mark. 4.5" dia. Perfect. £90/110. $125/150.

Very good fruit bowl. Blue
mark. 8.5" dia. Perfect.
£250/280. $360/400.

Bowl in Desert Scene. Blue mark. 8.5"
dia. Good. £220/240. $320/350.

Bowl in Desert Scene. Blue mark. 6.75"
dia. Perfect. £160/180. $230/260.

Bowl in Desert Scene. Blue mark. 7.5"
dia. Perfect. £280/300. $400/425.

Cake plate on EPNS stand. Blue mark.
10" dia. Good. £30/40. £45/60.

Cake plate on EPNS stand. Blue mark.
10" dia. Good. £40/50. $60/70.

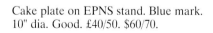

Fruit bowl with EPNS rim in Desert Scene. Blue mark. 10" dia. Good. £120/140. $175/210.

Butter dish with cover but missing insert on EPNS stand. Blue mark. Dish 5" dia. Good. £60/80. $85/115.

Bonbon dish in Desert Scene on EPNS stand. Blue mark. Dish 6.5" dia. Stand 7.25" high. Perfect. £180/200. $260/290.

Fruit dish in Desert Scene on EPNS stand. Blue mark. Dish 9.75" dia. Perfect. £280/300. $400/425.

155

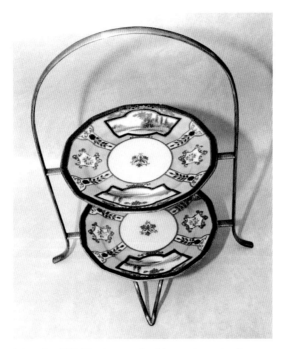

Two tier EPNS cake stand with good scenic plates. Blue mark. Plates 6.5" dia. Good. £130/150. $190/220.

Sweetmeat dish on EPNS stand. Blue mark. Dish 6.75" dia. Overall height 8". Perfect. £180/200. $260/290.

Right: Sweetmeat dish on EPNS stand. Blue mark. Dish 5.75" dia. Overall height 7.5". Perfect. £160/180. $230/260.

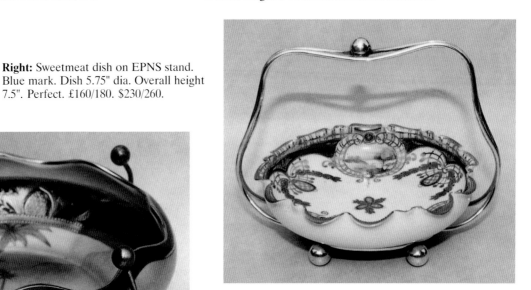

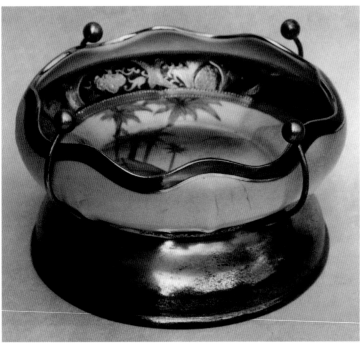

Fruit bowl on EPNS stand. Blue mark. Bowl 8.5" dia. Overall height 7.75". Perfect. £280/300. $400/425.

Right: Butter dish in Desert Scene on EPNS stand, insert missing. Blue mark. Dish 3.25" dia., stand 6.5" high. Good. £250/280. $360/400.

156

Chapter Eleven

Dressing Table Sets

Dressing table sets, known in America simply as "Dresser Sets," were an integral part of the equipment in any ladies boudoir from mid-Victorian times until the early 1950s, with the peak of popularity between 1880 and around 1930. There is no "standard" dressing table set, and therefore many, many variations exist, all of which could be worthy of the name. There are, however, a number of component parts that would be part of the set, in any of an almost infinite number of combinations. These components seem to have been put together to suit individual taste to make the set as simple or as comprehensive as required.

Perfume or Cologne Bottles

Perfume bottles, either individually or as a pair, were globular in shape, and came complete with stoppers. Pairs were normally mirrored and the stoppers were usually gilded. Cologne bottles were of a different shape, and could be of tall, hexagonal form, although there are examples in the form of small ewers. The same comments apply in terms of decoration and pairs.

Candlesticks

Candlesticks were originally an essential component of early dressing table sets, but continued after the advent of proper domestic lighting very much as decorative items. Candlesticks were sold as individual decorative items or sets, but the discrete version was usually anything up to 12 inches in height. The candlesticks for use with a dressing table set are usually in the region of 5 inches in height, and, again will be a single item or a pair, usually mirrored.

Trinket Pots & Covers

There is a huge variety of trinket pots and covers, and at least two or three were found in most dressing table sets. Normally there were two sizes, and a typical set would have a large size, around 3.5 inches diameter, and two smaller pots, around 2.5 inches diameter. The shape was usually round, however there are also hex-agonal and square versions, although these are not so common. In the better, higher quality sets, trinket pots and covers stood on legs, making them very decorative. The two shapes were round, on three legs, and oblong with four. Sizes were still similar to the standard pots, 2.5 inches diameter and around 3.5 inches for the larger version.

Hair Receivers

Hair receivers were generally circular in form, and could stand on three legs, but all had a circular hole in the cover. The fashion was to save hair that came from hairbrushes and combs for use in lockets or embroidery, and loose hair was simply pulled from the brush or comb, and pushed down into the hair receiver with a finger. Generally hair receivers were of the larger 3.5 inch size.

Ring Holders

Ring holders normally were in two styles, one shaped as an open hand, the other as a form of stylized tree, and could be on a circular, hexagonal, or square base. They were designed to hold rings, small broaches, cufflinks, and collar studs.

Hatpin Holders

Hatpins were an essential fashion accessory when most women wore hats every day. The hatpin holder was a handy receptacle for the lady's collection, and holders would hold up to a dozen or more. The shape was usually a cylindrical truncated cone, however there was a rarer shape which incorporated a tray base.

Trinket Trays

Trinket trays were often included in a set, again to hold small dressing items such as broaches, collar studs, and cufflinks. The tray was usually oblong or octagonal, although there were some examples on small legs, which were usually circular with a diameter of around 3 inches.

Base Trays

Collecting Dressing Table Sets

All the items in the dressing table set were designed to sit on a base tray. These trays were of various shapes, the commonest being an oval of around 8.5 inches diameter, but square examples and large oblong octagonal shapes can be found with diameters of up to 11 inches.

Dressing table sets, in common with other Noritake "sets," are very hard to assemble by obtaining the individual components over a period, but not impossible. It is, generally best to buy a complete set, but as the range of mold shapes is comparatively limited, finding the odd pieces to complete a partial set can be done, with patience. As with all items which were originally designed for day to day use, damage is a major consideration, especially to the covers on trinket pots and hair receivers.

Trinket pot and cover. Blue mark. 2.75" dia. Good. £15/20. $20/30.

Trinket pot and cover. Blue mark. 2.75" dia. Good. £50/60. £70/85.

Trinket pot and cover. Blue mark. 2.75" dia. Good. £15/20. $20/30.

Trinket pot and cover. Blue mark. 2.75" dia. Good. £50/60. $70/85.

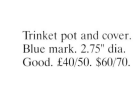

Trinket pot and cover. Blue mark. 2.75" dia. Good. £40/50. $60/70.

Trinket pot and cover with luster finish. Blue mark. 2.5" dia. Perfect. £20/25. $30/35.

et set. Blue mark. Small pots 2" dia. Large pot 3.5" dia.
ed trinket tray, 4" dia. Good. The set, £200/250. $290/360.

Good jewelled trinket pot and cover.
Blue mark. 2.75" dia. Perfect. £80/90.
$115/125.

Trinket pot and cover. Blue mark. 2.75" dia.
Good. £65/75. $90/110.

Good scenic trinket pot and cover. Blue mark.
2.75" dia. Perfect. £130/160. $190/230.

Trinket pot and cover. Blue mark. 2" dia.
Perfect. £75/85. $110/120.

Scenic trinket pot and cover. Blue mark. 2.75" dia.
Good. £70/90. $100/125.

Trinket pot and cover in Desert Scene.
Blue mark. 2.75" dia. Good. £110/130.
$160/190.

Square scenic trinket pot and cover. Blue mark. 3"
dia. x 3" high. Good. £90/110. $125/160.

Trinket pot and cover. Blue mark. 2.75" dia. Good.
£40/50. $60/70.

Hexagonal trinket pot and cover. Blue mark.
2.75" dia. x 3" high. Good. £80/100. $115/145.

Very decorative trinket pot and cover. Blue
mark. 3" dia. x 3.5" high. Good. £100/125.
$145/175.

Heart shaped trinket pot and cover.
Blue mark. 1.75" x 2.5". Good.
£55/65. $80/90.

Pair of hexagonal trinket pots and covers. Blue mark. 3" dia. x 32" high. Good. The pair, £110/130. $160/190.

Hair receiver. Blue mark. 3" dia. Good. £25/35. $35/50.

Pair of hexagonal trinket pots and covers. Blue mark. 2.75" dia. x 2.75" high. Good. The pair, £110/130. $160/190.

Hair receiver. Blue mark. 3.75" dia. Good. £75/85. $110/120.

Hair receiver. Blue mark. 3" dia. Good. £25/35. $35/50.

Pedestal trinket pot and cover . Blue mark. 2" dia. x 2.5" high. £25/35. $35/50.

Trinket pot and cover on three legs.
Blue mark. 2.5" dia. x 2" high.
Perfect. £55/65. $80/90.

"Piano Stool" trinket pot and cover. Green mark. 4" l. x 2.5" w.
x 2.5" h. Good. £120/140. $175/210.

"Piano Stool" trinket pot and cover. Blue
mark. 3" l. x 2" w. x 2.25" h. Good. £75/85.
$110/120.

"Piano Stool" trinket pot and cover in Desert Scene.
Matte finish. Blue mark. 4" l. x 2.5" w. x 2.5" h. Perfect.
£150/180. $220/260.

"Piano Stool" trinket pot and cover. Blue mark. 3" l. x 2" w.
x 2.25" h. Perfect. £130/150. $190/220.

Trinket pot and cover on three legs. 4" dia. x 3.75" high.
Good. £70/90. $100/125.

162

Trinket pot and cover on three legs. Blue mark. 4" dia. x 3.75" high. Perfect. £120/140. $175/210.

Hair receiver on three legs in Desert Scene. 4" dia. x 3" high. Perfect. £175/200. $250/290.

Trinket pot and cover on three legs in Desert Scene. 4" dia. x 3" high. Perfect. £175/200. $250/290.

Hair receiver on three legs in Desert Scene. Blue mark. 4" dia. x 2.5" high. Perfect. £190/210. $265/300.

Trinket pot and cover on three legs in Desert Scene. Blue mark. 4" dia. x 2.5" high. Perfect. £190/210. $265/300.

Trinket tray on three squat legs in Desert Scene. Blue mark. 4.5" dia. Good. £110/130. $160/190.

Powder bowl and cover. Blue mark. 5.75" dia. Perfect. £240/260. $350/375.

Powder bowl and cover. Blue mark. 7.25" dia. Good. £90/110. $125/160.

Good scenic powder bowl and cover. Blue mark. 7.25" dia. Perfect. £425/475. $595/675.

Powder bowl and cover in Desert Scene with matte finish. Blue mark. 5.75" dia. Perfect. £350/400. $495/560.

Scenic powder bowl and cover. Blue mark. 5.75" dia. Good. £170/190. $245/265.

Powder bowl and cover in Desert Scene. Blue mark. 5.75" dia. Perfect. £325/350. $460/495.

Cologne bottle. Blue mark. 5.5" high. Good. £110/130. $160/190.

Pair of cologne bottles modeled as miniature ewers. Blue mark. 6" high. Perfect. £225/250. $325/360. Each.

Pair of hexagonal cologne bottles. Blue mark. 5.5" high. Good. The pair, £280/320. $400/450.

Perfume bottle and stopper. Blue mark. 4.75" high. Perfect. £200/250. $290/360.

Good perfume bottle and stopper. Blue mark. 4.75" high. Perfect. £225/275. $325/400.

Pair of perfume bottles and stoppers. Blue mark. 4.75" high. Good. The pair, £300/330. $425/475.

Perfume bottle and stopper. Green mark. 4.75" high. Good. £120/140. $175/210.

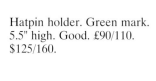

Hatpin holder. Green mark. 5.5" high. Good. £90/110. $125/160.

Hatpin holder with trinket tray. Blue mark. 5.5" high. Good. £100/120. $145/175.

Scenic perfume bottle and stopper. Blue mark. 4.75" high. Perfect. £225/275. $325/400.

Open top hatpin
holder (possibly a spill
holder). Blue mark. 5"
high. Good. £40/60.
$60/85.

Dresser tray. Blue mark. 8.5" dia. Good. £70/90. $100/125.

Hatpin holder in Desert
Scene. Blue mark. 5.5" high.
Good. £120/140. $175/210.

Unusual shape
hatpin holder in
Desert Scene.
Matte finish. Blue
mark. 5.5" high.
£100/125. $145/180.

Dresser tray. Blue mark. 8.5" dia. Good. £70/90. $100/125.

Octagonal dresser tray with scenic cartouches. Blue mark. 13" dia. Good. £150/175. $220/255.

Dresser tray in Desert Scene. Blue mark. 8.5" dia. Good. £180/220. $260/320.

Pair of candlesticks in Desert Scene. Blue mark. 5.75" high. Good. The pair, £250/275. $360/400.

Ring tree. Blue mark. 3.5" dia. Good.
£40/60. $60/85.

Hexagonal ring tree. Blue mark. 3.25" dia.
Good. £70/80. $100/115.

Ring tree in Desert Scene. Blue mark. 3.5" dia. Good. £80/90.
$115/125.

Dressing table set in Desert Scene. Blue mark. Good. £1000/1200. $1400/1700.

Dressing table set in Desert Scene. Blue mark. Good. £1000/1200. $1400/1700.

Dressing table set. Blue mark. Good. £900/1100. $1250/1550.

Chapter Twelve
Miscellaneous Items

In this chapter you will find all of the items and sets that don't really fit into any of the other categories. There are items of kitchenalia, cruet sets, and components, jugs, ewers, and biscuit barrels. There are a number of items pertaining to smoking such as ash trays and humidors. The American export wares include a large number of smokers requisites, which have become very collectible in the United States. In Europe, where wood or silver were the preferred mediums for cigarette boxes and associated items, this was not such a big market so this type of ware is comparatively rare, especially the more decorative pieces.

There are also a number of potpourri containers, that were the forerunners of air fresheners. A potpourri container should consist of three component parts, a base container that actually contained the scented material, a pierced lid, and an inner cover which sits between the base and the pierced lid. This inner cover is quite often missing, which will affect the value of the piece.

Collecting unusual and rare items can be very rewarding, but can involve a lot of patience to wait for the right piece, and a lot of searching in antique shops and antique fairs.

Scenic mustard pot and cover. Blue mark. Good. £20/30. $30/45.

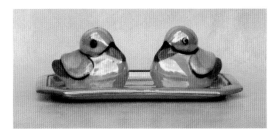

Figural salt and pepper in luster glaze on a matching tray. Blue mark. Perfect. £70/80. $100/115.

Figural salt cellar in luster glaze, formed as a clown. "Made in Japan" in red. 2.25" high. Perfect. £25/35. $35/50.

Pepper pot and salt dip in luster glaze. This set would normally be on a matching tray. Blue mark. Perfect. £40/50. $60/70.

Boiled egg set consisting of egg cup and miniature individual salt and pepper on a matching tray, all in luster glaze. Blue mark. Perfect. £50/60. $70/85.

Unusual floral themed cruet set in luster glazes. Blue mark. Perfect. £120/140. $175/210.

Cruet set in Basket of Flowers pattern. Green mark. Perfect. £55/65. $80/90.

Tall salt and pepper in Desert Scene. Blue mark. 4.5" high. Good. £70/80. $100/115.

Breakfast preserve set comprising salt, pepper, butter dish, and preserve pot with cover and spoon, all on a matching tray. Green mark. Good. £120/140. $175/210.

Salt and pepper in Basket of Flowers pattern. This set carries an example of a partial backstamp. The full set illustrated in this pattern has the green mark on the tray; however, these smaller pieces do not have the space for a full backstamp so carry only "Made in Japan" in red. Good. £20/25. $30/35.

Biscuit barrel and cover. Blue mark. 7.5" high. Good.
£220/240. $320/350.

Scenic biscuit barrel. Blue mark. 6.75" high. Good. £250/300.
$360/425.

Biscuit barrel with lion moldings in Desert Scene. These moldings
are designed to take the end hooks of a cane handle, which is
usually missing. Blue mark. 6.75" high. Good. £250/300. $360/425.

Biscuit barrel. Blue mark. 7.5" high. Perfect. £220/250.
$320/360.

Biscuit barrel. Blue mark. 6.75" high. Good. £140/160. $210/230.

Biscuit barrel with EPNS lid and handle in Desert Scene. Blue mark. 6.5" high (excluding handle). Good. £160/180. $230/260.

Biscuit barrel. Blue mark. 6.5" high. Good. £140/160. $210/230.

Biscuit barrel. Blue mark. 7.5" high. Perfect. £240/260. $350/375.

Ashtray. Green mark. 3.25" dia. Good. £10/15. $15/20.

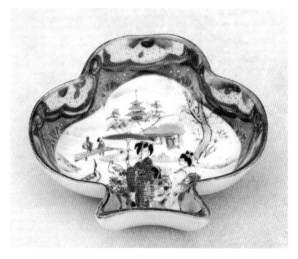

Ashtray in Geisha Girl pattern. Blue mark. 3.5" dia. Good. £20/25. $30/35.

Ashtray in Art Deco style. This and the three following pictures form a set of four ashtrays that have American export patterns, but all bear the European export green mark, thus making them very rare pieces. 4.75" x 4". Perfect. £90/100. $125/145.

Ashtray. Green mark. 3.25" dia. Good. £10/15. $15/20.

Ashtray. Green mark. 4.25" x 3.75". Perfect. £90/100. $125/145.

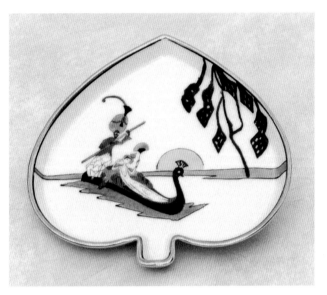

Ashtray. Green mark. 4.5" x 4.25". Perfect. £90/100. $125/145.

Ashtray. Green mark. 4.25" x 4". Perfect. £90/100. $125/145.

Humidor with a continuous hunting scene, relief moulded with jewelling and gilded highlights. This is a classic American export item which bears the European export blue mark making this piece a rarity. 5.75" dia., 5.5" high. Perfect. £475/525. $675/725.

Illustration of the rear of the humidor showing the continuous scene.

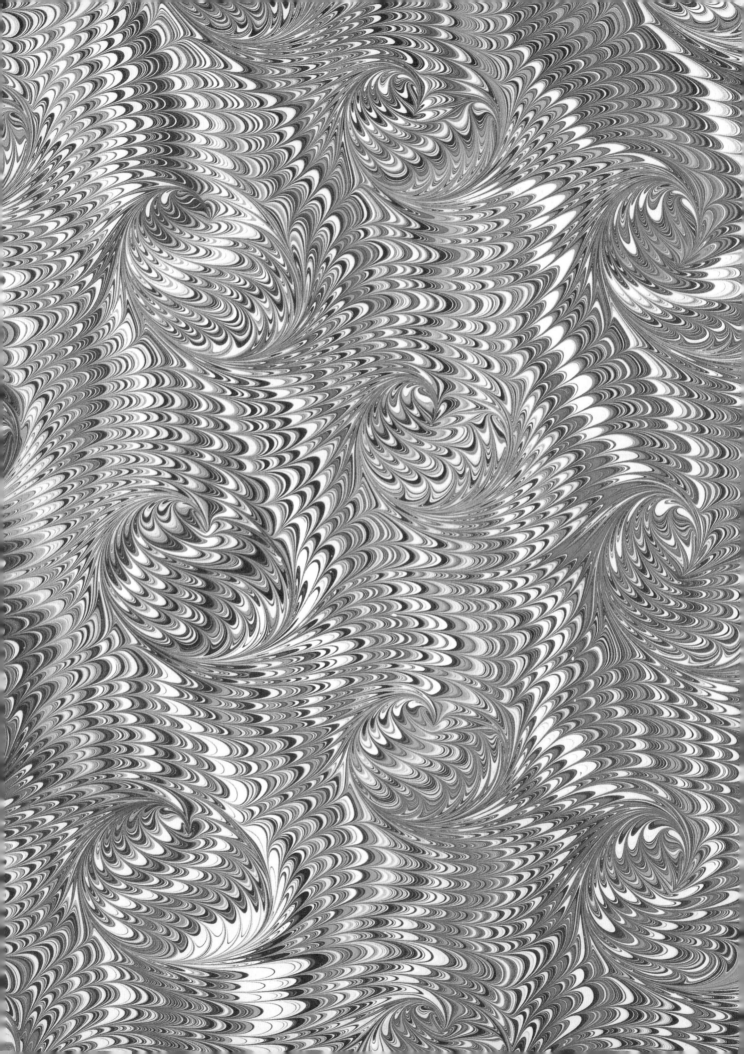